A MANUAL
FOR WRITERS

*of Term Papers, Theses,
and Dissertations*

A MANUAL
FOR WRITERS
of Term Papers, Theses,
and Dissertations

By

KATE L. TURABIAN

Phoenix Books

THE UNIVERSITY OF CHICAGO PRESS

CHICAGO AND LONDON

THE UNIVERSITY OF CHICAGO PRESS, CHICAGO & LONDON

The University of Toronto Press, Toronto 5, Canada

Foreword

This manual is designed to serve as a guide to suitable style in the presentation of formal papers—term papers, reports, articles, theses, dissertations—both in scientific and in non-scientific fields. While the ideas, the findings, and the conclusions put forth in the paper are of primary importance, their consideration by the reader depends in large measure upon an orderly presentation, well documented and free of mechanical flaws.

In the main, the manual is addressed to the writers of the papers, who have the major responsibility for their organization and form in general. The section on typing is addressed especially to the typists who have the responsibility for preparing the final copies, and much of that section, which deals with the mechanics of typing, may be of no interest to the writers, unless it be to those who expect to prepare their own final typescripts. Professional typists, and secretaries who now and again are called upon to whip into shape a report in which only the bare facts are ready for presentation when it reaches their desks, may well find the greater part of the manual useful in their task.

It must be pointed out that no suggestions are given here about *how to write*. The assumption is that, if the writer feels the need of further training in composition, he will consult a reliable up-to-date work on English composition.[1]

In general, the style here recommended is that of the University of Chicago Press as set forth in *A Manual of Style* (11th ed.; Chicago:

[1] Two may be mentioned: Porter G. Perrin, *Writer's Guide and Index to English* (rev. ed., 1950; Chicago: Scott, Foresman & Co., 1942); and Charles Carpenter Fries, *American English Grammar* (New York: Appleton-Century-Crofts, 1940).

University of Chicago Press, 1949) and exhibited in its publications, both books and scholarly journals. In some scientific fields the specific form of literature citation used by a leading journal in a field not covered by periodicals issued by the University of Chicago Press is recommended. Although not all areas in scientific fields are represented in the examples cited, in their main outlines the examples illustrate the various accepted usages in scientific writing.

The writer of this manual is greatly indebted to the University of Chicago Press for its generous co-operation in making this publication possible. Two members of the staff of the Press she would mention especially: Miss Mary D. Alexander, Production Editor, from whom she learned the first rudiments of bibliographic style and upon whom she has placed constant reliance for answers to thorny questions; and Mr. Morton Grodzins, Professor of Political Science in the University and formerly Editor of the Press, who encouraged the writer to undertake the present revision and expansion.

Miss Winifred Ver Nooy, formerly Reference Librarian of the University of Chicago Libraries, furnished valuable suggestions for the section of public documents and gave much time and thought to locating examples of the more difficult forms.

Various members of the Department of English have offered useful suggestions and provided concrete examples.

Finally, students and typists, with whom the writer has worked in close contact through their use of the parent manual, have suggested additions and alterations which it is hoped will increase the usefulness of the present work to new generations of students.

Contents

I

The Format of the Paper

1. Normally, a paper[1] is made up of three main parts: the preliminaries, the text, and the reference matter. In a long paper each of these main parts may consist of several sections (see below); but in a short paper there may be nothing more than a title page and text, the latter with or without subheadings, tables, illustrations, as the topic and treatment may require. The inclusion of a table or two, an illustration or two, does not automatically call for a list of tables and a list of illustrations; and for some papers a table of contents may have little value. These are matters, however, that must be left to the good sense of the writer, who should know best what arrangements are suitable for his particular piece of work.

The *order* of the following outline, regardless of the parts that may be omitted, must be observed.

a) The preliminaries, composed of
    (1) Title page (followed by a blank page).
    (2) Preface, including acknowledgments; or acknowledgments alone unless these appear as the final paragraph in the thesis.
    (3) Table of contents.
    (4) List of tables.
    (5) List of illustrations.
b) The text, composed of
    (1) Introduction.
    (2) Half-title page.

The term "paper" is used throughout this manual to refer alike to term papers, reports, theses, and dissertations except in matters relating specifically to the latter.

(3) Main body of the paper, usually consisting of well-defined divisions, such as chapters or their equivalents.[2]

c) *The reference matter*, composed of
   (1) Appendix.[2]
   (2) Bibliography.[2]
   (The order of these may be reversed.)

[2] If half-title pages are placed before groups of chapters, they should also be placed before the Appendix (or Appendixes) and the Bibliography.

II

The Preliminaries

2. *Title page.*—Most universities and colleges have their own style of title page for theses and dissertations, and this should be followed exactly in matters of content and spacing. For term papers and reports, if a sample sheet is not provided, a title page might logically include the name of the university or college (usually centered at the top of the sheet), the exact title of the paper, the course, the date, and the name of the writer—all suitably capitalized, centered, and spaced upon the page.

3. *Half-title page.*—Although not placed or numbered with the preliminaries, the half-title page is logically mentioned here. The Part number and title of the part it precedes are centered upon the page, typed in capital letters throughout. It is assigned a page number appropriate to its place in the paper, but the number does not appear on the page.

4. *Preface or acknowledgments.*—A preface should not be confused with an introduction. Included in the preface are such matters as the writer's reasons for making the study, its scope and purpose, the aids afforded him in the process of the research and writing by institutions and persons. If the writer thinks he has nothing significant to say about the study that is not covered in the main body of the paper and wishes only to acknowledge the assistance of various kinds he has received, the heading

"Acknowledgments" rather than "Preface" should be used for this section.

The heading is typed in capital letters throughout and is centered at least two inches below the top of the page—more if the text is short. The whole should be approximately centered upon the sheet.

5. *Table of contents.*—The heading "TABLE OF CONTENTS," or if preferred simply "CONTENTS," is typed in capital letters throughout and centered at least two inches from the top of the sheet. Whether the heading should be dropped more than two inches depends upon the length of the table. The entire body of typed matter should be centered upon the page; that is, the blank space above and below the typing should be approximately equal—always allowing, however, no less than two inches at the top of the page.

The table of contents shows the chapter numbers in capital Roman numerals, and the chapter headings in capital letters throughout, with a line of spaced periods (i.e., period leaders) run from the last letter of the heading to the page number. The word "Chapter" in small letters is typed above the column of chapter numbers, and the word "Page" above the column of page numbers.

Whether the table of contents should give the subtitles below the chapter titles depends upon the writer in most cases. He may feel it desirable to present a more or less complete outline; he may think that only subtitles of the first order are necessary. If they are included, the subtitles of each order are indented to the right of the order preceding. Those of the first order are typed in capital and small letters (i.e., the first and last words and all nouns, pronouns, adjectives, adverbs, and verbs capitalized); those of succeeding orders—if they appear—are typed in small letters except for the first word and proper nouns and proper adjectives. Double-space between chapter headings and between chapter headings and subheadings; single-space between subheadings. Chapter titles and all subtitles should correspond exactly with those appearing in the body of the paper. (An exception is made, of course, for the occasional paper in which the table of contents may indicate subdivisions that are not given subtitles in the text.)

(A sample table of contents is shown on p 98.)

6. *List of tables.*—The arrangement and position of the heading "LIST OF TABLES" should be the same as for the table of contents. The list of tables shows the table numbers in Arabic numerals and the titles in capital and small letters (i.e., the first and last words and all nouns, pronouns, adjectives, adverbs, and verbs capitalized), with period leaders extending from the last letter of the title to the page number. The word "Table" in small letters is typed above the column of table numbers, and the word "Page" above the column of page numbers.

(A sample list of tables is shown on p. 100.)

7. *List of illustrations.*—The list of illustrations should be in the same general form as the list of tables. Plate numbers should be designated with capital Roman numerals; figure numbers, with Arabic numerals. If the legends beneath the illustrations themselves are long, a shortened form in the list of illustrations is usually permissible. In some fields (Geography is one) the shortened form in the list of illustrations is not allowed. If, however, a descriptive or explanatory statement in addition to the title appears with the illustration, this statement should be omitted from the list of illustrations.

(A sample list of illustrations is shown on p. 100.)

III

The Text

8. *Introduction.*—The text ordinarily begins with an introduction, which may be Chapter I. If it is short, the writer may prefer to head it simply "Introduction," and reserve the more formal heading "Chapter" for the longer sections of which the main body of the paper is composed. But the Introduction, whether it is called Chapter I or not, is the first major division of the text, not the last of the preliminaries, as is sometimes supposed. Thus the first page of the Introduction is page 1 (Arabic numeral) of the paper.

9. *Chapters or their equivalents.*—The main body of the paper is usually divided into chapters, each chapter having a title and each beginning on a new page. For a short paper some writers prefer to omit the word "Chapter" and to use merely Roman numerals in sequence before the headings of the several main divisions of the paper. On the other hand, for a long paper some writers like to group related chapters into "Parts," with or without individual titles (see sample, p. 98). Each Part, then, is indicated by a half-title page immediately preceding the chapters of which it is composed.

10. *Sections and subsections.*—In many papers the chapters or their equivalents are divided into sections, and sometimes further into one or more series of subsections, each preceded by a subtitle. The plan for the display of subtitles depends upon the number of series of subsections to be shown. The style of heading with the greatest attention value must be given to the sections, and headings in a descending order of attention value to the subsections and sub-subsections. It is agreed that centered headings have greater attention value than side headings and that underlined headings have greater attention value than those not underlined. Supposing, then, that five ranks of subtitles were required, the following scheme would be appropriate:

a) Centered heading, underlined.

b) Centered heading, not underlined.

c) Side heading (that is, flush with the left margin), underlined.

d) Side heading, not underlined.

e) Paragraph heading (that is, a heading run into the paragraph, followed by a period and a dash), underlined.

If fewer than five ranks are required, they might be selected in any suitable *descending order* as indicated in *a*) to *e*) above.

Capital and small letters (i.e., the first and last words and all nouns, pronouns, adjectives, adverbs, and verbs capitalized) should be used for centered headings; capital letters for the first word and for proper nouns and adjectives and small letters for the remaining words in side headings and paragraph headings.

11. *Titles in text.*—The same rules should be followed in text as in footnotes for the capitalization and underlining of certain titles and the "quoting" of others (see secs. 26, 27, and 28, pp 28–29).

12. *Quotations.*—In general, quotations should correspond exactly with the originals in wording, spelling, and punctuation. Exceptions to this rule are discussed in *c*), *d*), and *e*) below.

a) *Prose.*—Short direct prose quotations should be incorporated into the text of the paper and enclosed in double quotation marks. But, in general, a prose quotation of two or more sentences which *at the same time* runs to four or more typewritten lines should be set off from the text in single spacing and indented in its entirety four spaces from the left marginal line, with no quotation marks at beginning and end. Exceptions to this rule are allowable when for purposes of emphasis or of comparison it is desirable to single-space and indent quotations less than four typewritten lines in length. Paragraph indention in the original text should be indicated by an eight-space indention from the left marginal line, as for a paragraph in the text of the paper. (See sample page, p. 102.) Spacing between paragraphs taken from the same work should be single. But when passages are quoted from different authors or from different works of the same author, and they are not separated by intervening original matter, the passages should be separated by double spaces.

b) *Poetry.*—Citations of poetry two or more lines in length should be set off from text in single spacing and centered upon the page. No quotation marks should be used at beginning and end except when quoting passages from different authors or different works of the same author, uninterrupted by intervening original matter.

c) *Ellipsis.*—For omissions within a sentence three spaced periods (spaces before and after as well as between) should be used:

        "What we require to be taught . . . is to be our own
    teachers."

If there is punctuation preceding the ellipsis, the mark is put immediately next to the word:

> "If we care to give the name of mystical to the thought
> of what is beyond all experience, . . . it is not worth while ob-
> jecting to the expression."

If a new sentence follows an ellipsis, a sentence period should precede the ellipsis whether it was in the original or not:

> "Our only test . . . is what is actually desired. . . . He
> has attempted to establish the identity of the good with the de-
> sired."

The omission of a complete paragraph (or more) in a prose quotation, or of a line (or more) in a verse quotation, should be indicated by a single line of spaced periods:

> Hark! hark! the sweet vibrating lyre
> Sets my attentive soul on fire;
> . . . .
> And the more slow and solemn bass
> Adds charm to charm and grace to grace.

In French and in Spanish text, omissions within a sentence are indicated by three periods without space between, but with space both before and after them. If the omission follows the end of a sentence, the three periods follow the sentence period:

> "Masquant leur égoïsme sous le voile de la philosophie,
> ils affichaient ses maximes ... pour séduire le vulgaire et bâtir
> leur fortune aux dépens de sa crédulité. ... Voilà les égoïstes
> qui déshonorent la philosophie."

In Italian text, any omission should be indicated by four unspaced periods followed by a space. Any punctuation mark immediately preceding the omission takes the place of the first period:

> "Piano!... Ho sentito muovere de la.... Dev'essera
> là.... cosa dell'ingegnere...."

Omissions in German, Latin, and Greek quoted matter may be indicated in the same way as in English.

d) *Interpolations.*—Any interpolation into a quotation made by the writer of the paper must be placed between square brackets [ ]. Parentheses may *not* be substituted; if the typewriter has no brackets, they must be inserted in ink. *Sic* (Latin, "so"; always underlined) is a common interpolation used to assure the reader that the faulty spelling or faulty logic was in the original.

> "When the fog lifted, they were delighted to see that the country was heavily timbered and emmence [<u>sic</u>] numbers of fowl flying in every direction."

The use of *sic* should not be overdone, however. Quotations from a work of the sixteenth century, for example, or from obviously archaic or illiterate writing, should not be strewn with *sic*'s.

Interpolations for purposes of correction and clarification are illustrated in the following:

> "As the Italian [Englishman] Dante Gabriel Rossetti has said, . . ."

> "Between the problem of the traumatic neurosis [the psychological event] and that of Jewish monotheism [the historical event] there is a complete series of correspondences."

e) *Other permissible changes.*—Apart from ellipsis and interpolation in quoted matter, the following changes from the originals are common practice:

(1) The first word of a quotation is not capitalized if it is related grammatically to what precedes, even though in the original it begins a sentence:

> The Act provided that "the General Counsel of the Board shall exercise general supervision." [In the original "the" is the beginning of a sentence.]

Conversely, if the quotation is not incorporated grammatically into the text sentence, the first word is capitalized even though it may not be in the original quotation:

> The following day Sand reported: "With Pebble soliciting members on the side, it was imperative that the meeting be no longer delayed." [In the original "With" occurs within a sentence and therefore is not capitalized.]

This rule should be followed both for quotations run into text and for those set off from text in single spacing.

(2) Since for a quotation run on in text double quotation marks are required at beginning and end, any internal double quotation marks in the original of the part quoted must be changed to single. But for a single-spaced, indented quotation, the marks used in the original are retained.

(3) Words not italicized in the original may be italicized (underlined) for emphasis desired by the writer of the paper. This change may be indicated to the reader in one of three ways:

(*a*) By a notation enclosed in square brackets placed immediately after the underlined words, as in the following:

> "This man described to me another large river beyond the Rocky Mountains; the southern branch [italics mine] of which he directed me to take."

(*b*) By a parenthetical note following the quotation, as:

> "This man described to me another large river beyond the Rocky Mountains; the southern branch of which he directed me to take." (Italics mine.)

(*c*) By a footnote. The second or third scheme is preferable when italics have been added at two or more points in a quotation.

(4) *Punctuation with the final quotation mark.*—Periods and commas should be put inside quotation marks (even though the quotation marks enclose only one letter or figure); semicolons and colons, outside. Question marks and exclamation marks should be put outside the quotation marks unless they are part of the matter quoted:

```
Does he precisely show "evil leading somehow to good"?
The question asked was:   "Can evil ever lead to good?"
```

Other general rules of punctuation are discussed in Appendix II, pages 91–97.

13. *Numbers.*—The general rule for ordinary text matter is to spell out numbers under three digits and to use numerals for those of three digits or more, but the exceptions to this rule are many.

Exceptions

a) In a group containing both numbers under and numbers over three digits, use Arabic numerals for all.

b) In a technical or statistical discussion involving frequent use of numbers, use Arabic numerals for all.

c) For percentages, decimals, dates; street and telephone numbers; exact sums of money; numbers combined with abbreviations, use numerals.

d) For reference to parts of a work use numerals as follows:

(1) lower-case Roman numerals (i, ii, iv, x, etc.) to indicate book (in classical references), chapter, scene, canto, preliminary pages;

(2) capital Roman numerals (I, II, IV, X, etc.) to indicate volume, act, part, division, plate;

(3) Arabic numerals to indicate pages other than preliminaries, column, line, table, figure, and possibly other divisions.

e) Never begin a sentence with a numeral, even if there are numerals in the rest of the sentence. Either spell out the first number or, better, recast the sentence.

f) Spell out ordinals and fractions except when the fraction is part of a number of three digits or more:

```
nineteenth century                        one-tenth
Fifth Avenue                    But:  124-1/2
```

g) Spell out the time of day except when A.M. or P.M. is used:

```
The meeting was called for four o'clock.
The meeting was called for 9:30 A.M.
```

14. *Enumerations:*

a) *Run on in text.*—Numbers or letters used in enumerating items in text should be enclosed in parentheses:

```
Right:  The reasons for his resignation were three:  (1) advanced
        age, (2) failing health, (3) a desire to travel.
```

```
Wrong:  The reasons for his resignation were three:  1. advanced
        age, 2. failing health, 3. a desire to travel.
```

b) *Beginning a new line or paragraph.*—When each item in an enumeration begins a new line or paragraph, one of the following should be used:

```
    1.
    1)
or
    a)
```

For an enumeration without subdivisions, Arabic numerals followed by periods are preferred; the periods are always aligned.

```
8. Purchase of supplies.
9. Operation of physical plant.
10. Reduction in cost of collecting school funds.
```

c) *In outline form.*—For an outline or other enumeration having several subdivisions, the following scheme of notation and indentation should be used:

```
 I. Under the head of . . .
    A. Under . . .
       1. Under . . .
          a) Under . . .
             (1) Under . . .
                (a) Under . . .
                    i) Under . . .
                   ii) Under . . .

II. Under the head of . . .
    A. Under . . .
       1. Under . . .
          a) Under . . .
                              ETC.
```

15. *Spelling.*—In general, spelling, including hyphenation, should accord with the best American usage, and it must, of course, be consistent, except in quotations. The authority should be the latest edition of *Webster's New International Dictionary.*

a) *Possessive of proper names.*—Form the possessive of *one-syllable* proper names ending in *s* or another sibilant by adding an apostrophe and *s:*

```
Wells's novels           Marx's theories
Keats's poems            Jones's house
```

In names of *more than one syllable* ending in a sibilant, add the apostrophe only, except for names ending in a sibilant and *e:*

```
Praxiteles' sculpture    But: Horace's odes
Berlioz' music                Bernice's grades
```

Form the possessive plural of proper names by adding an apostrophe to the accepted form of the plural of the name (see *b* below):

The Millses' car	The Jenkinses' house
The Bentleys' dog	The McBains' farm

b) *Plural of proper names.*—Form the plural of proper names ending in a sibilant, except those ending with a sibilant and a final *e*, by adding *es;* others, by adding *s:*

the Rosses	the Marxes	the Costellos
the Jenkinses	the Joyces	the Audleys

16. *Division of words and other separations at ends of lines.*—In general, divide words at the ends of lines according to their syllabication as shown in Webster's Dictionary. Make the following exceptions, however:

a) *Never* make a one-letter division:

Wrong: a-mong   e-nough   u-nite   man-y

b) *Never* carry over *-ed* if the word is pronounced as one syllable:

Wrong: help-ed   vex-ed   climb-ed   pass-ed

c) *Never* divide the final syllables *-able* and *-ible*.

Wrong: converti-ble   reada-ble

d) *Never* divide the following suffixes:

-ceous	-cious	-sial	-tion
-cial	-geous	-sion	-tious
-cion	-gion	-tial	

e) Carry over *-ing* except when the ending consonant of the parent word is doubled before *-ing:*

will-ing   But: win-ning
spell-ing   and
                                control-ling

f) "When the ending-consonant sounds of the parent word belong to a syllable with a silent vowel, such consonants become part of the added syllable *-ing* or *-ed*" (*A Manual of Style*, p. 127):

```
han-dling      dwin-dling      bris-tling      chuck-ling
han-dled       dwin-dled       bris-tled       chuck-led
```

g) Do not divide a proper *name* unless it is one in which the correct division is obvious:

```
Wash-ing-ton    Dear-born    Went-worth    Jef-fer-son
```

h) The rules for dividing words in foreign languages are different from those in English (see *A Manual of Style*, pp. 129–34).

i) Do not divide (i.e., put in different lines) the initials of a name or the forename and the initial; the month and the day; or any such combinations as

```
£6 4s. 6d.          1406 B.C.          6:00 P.M.
```

17. *Abbreviations.*—In general, no abbreviations should be used in *the text*. Spell out all titles (except Mr., Messrs., Mrs., and their foreign equivalents; Dr., St., Rev., Hon. preceding personal names and Esq., Sr., and Jr. following names); names of states and months; expressions of dimension, weight, measure, distance; the words "chapter," "page," "column," "line," "volume," etc.; the words "Company" and "Brother" even when forming part of the name of a commercial firm. (But note that in footnotes, bibliography, and tables, abbreviations are not only permissible but are preferred.)

18. *Foreign words.*—Underline foreign words in English text, with the following exceptions:

Exceptions

a) The words in a quotation entirely in a foreign language are not underlined. In the following sentence, the words *le pragmatisme* are properly underlined, and the quotation, entirely in French, is properly not underlined.

The confusion of <u>le pragmatisme</u> is traced to the supposed failure to distinguish "les propriétés de la valeur en général" from the incidental.

b) Even a single foreign word is not underlined if it is quoted.

c) Foreign titles preceding proper names, and foreign names of persons, places, institutions, etc., are not underlined.

d) Foreign words which by continued use in English have become Anglicized are not underlined. Some of the more common of these are the following (consult Webster's Dictionary for others):

a posteriori	dilettante	per cent
a priori	entree	per se
ad infinitum	entrepreneur	pro rata
ante bellum	ex officio	regime
apropos	exposé	résumé
attaché	genre	role
bona fide	habeas corpus	status quo
carte blanche	laissez faire	subpoena
chargé d'affaires	milieu	tête-à-tête
cliché	mores	versus
communiqué	naïveté	vice versa
coup d'état	par excellence	vis-à-vis
debris	per annum	visé
denouement	per capita	Weltanschauung

With their adoption into the English language, some foreign words, as, e.g., "denouement," "entree," "regime," "role," have dropped the accent marks proper to their native forms. But the greater number retain the marks, and they must be inserted into the typed copy by hand if the typewriter is not equipped with them.

IV

Footnotes

19. *Their use.*—Footnotes have four main uses: (*a*) to cite the authority for statements in text—specific facts or opinions as well as exact quotations;[1] (*b*) to make incidental comments upon, to amplify or to qualify textual discussion—in short, to provide a place for material which the writer thinks it worthwhile to include but which he feels would disrupt the flow of thought if introduced into the text; (*c*) to make cross-references; (*d*) to make acknowledgments. Footnotes, then, are of two kinds, *reference* (*a* and *c* above), and *content* (*b* and *d* above). A content footnote may also include one or more references, as will be seen in the examples (sec. 48, p. 48). Interpretations and examples of footnote form are given in the following pages.

20. *Footnote numbers.*—The place in text at which a footnote is introduced, whether of the reference or of the content type, should be marked with an Arabic numeral—unembellished with parentheses, brackets, slashes, or any form of punctuation—elevated slightly above the line (but never a full space above it), and set after punctuation, if any. It should follow the passage to which it refers. If the passage is an exact quotation, the foot-

---

[1] Such authority is usually a written source, published or unpublished. When a general rather than a specific term must be used to refer to such a source, it is called in this manual a "work"; or, where its form needs to be more clearly indicated, a "whole work" or a "whole published work" to refer to a separate publication, and a "part" or a "component part" to refer to some division of the whole.

note number comes at the end of the quotation, not after the author's name or at the end of the textual matter introducing the quotation.

Footnote numbers should follow each other in numerical order on the page. They may begin with "1" (a small "1," not a capital "I," is used for the Arabic numeral one) on each page, or with "1" at the beginning of each chapter, or they may run in one series through the entire paper. There are possible complications in use of the last two schemes, however, since if it was found that a note had been omitted, or that one should be deleted, it would be necessary to renumber the footnotes from the point of the desired change to the end of the chapter or of the paper. The insertion of a note numbered, e.g., "1a" is not permissible, and the omission of a number likewise is not permissible.

21. *Position of footnotes.*—All footnotes should be arranged in numerical order at the foot of the page, and there must be the same number of footnotes as there are footnote numbers in the text. Specific directions for the typing of footnotes and for their correct placement on the page are given in Appendix I (pp. 83–90).

REFERENCE FOOTNOTES

FIRST, FULL REFERENCES

22. *Basic style.*—The first time a work is mentioned, the footnote should be given in complete form; that is, it not only should include the author's name, the title, and the volume and/or page number, but it should give the facts of publication as well. Thereafter the full form ordinarily is not repeated. Proper styles of footnote entries for subsequent references to works once cited in full are discussed on pages 44–47.

With some exceptions, such as legal, classical, and biblical references and references in scientific papers and to some classes of public documents (all discussed hereafter), reference footnotes citing a published work the first time are arranged and punctuated as indicated below. Although not every entry will include all the items of information mentioned, the order should be maintained regardless of the items omitted. The source of the information, except the page number, should be the title page of the book.

a) For a book:

    (1) Name of author, with forename or initials first; the family name followed by a comma.

    (2) Title of the book, underlined, followed by a comma. (But note that the comma follows the parenthesis if the "facts of publication" come immediately after the title.)

    (3) Name of editor or translator (if any).

    (4) Facts of publication, consisting of

        (*a*) total number of volumes (if necessary), followed by a semicolon;

        (*b*) number of the edition (if necessary), followed by a semicolon;

        (*c*) series title (if any), followed by a semicolon;

        (*d*) place of publication, followed by a colon;

        (*e*) name of publishing agency, followed by a comma;

        (*f*) date of publication.

Group all the elements under (4) within parentheses and place a comma after the final parenthesis.

    (5) Volume number (if necessary), in capital Roman numerals, followed by a comma.

    (6) Page number or numbers, followed by a period.

b) *For an article in a periodical:*

(1) Same as *a*, (1) above.

(2) Title of the article, placed between quotation marks, with a comma before the final quotation mark. Name of the periodical, underlined and followed by a comma.

(3) Usually non-existent.

(4) Not usually given, except for the date of publication, which for a periodical is closely related to the volume number and is mentioned under (5).

(5) Volume number, written in capital Roman numerals, followed by month and year; these last separated by a comma and placed between parentheses, with a comma following the second parenthesis.

(6) Page number or numbers, followed by a period.

c) Under their separate heads, all the foregoing will now be discussed in detail.

(1) *Name of author.*—Give the author's name in normal order —Robert John Blank—and follow with a comma. In general, give the forenames, not initials only, unless the title page or the byline at the head of the article gives only initials. Titles such as "Doctor," "Professor," "President"; the author's position, degrees held, etc., should be omitted unless their inclusion is of special significance in connection with the subject under discussion.

If the title page mentions no author, or if it indicates that the work is anonymous, and the authorship of the work has been definitely established, the author's name may be enclosed in brackets and placed before the title of the work (see example *f*, p. 32).

Similarly, if the title page bears a pseudonym known to be that of a certain author, the real name, placed between brackets, follows the pseudonym (see example *g*, p. 32).

If a pseudonym is indicated as such on the title page, the abbreviation "pseud." (in parentheses) follows the name.

If pseudonymity is not indicated on the title page but it is nevertheless an established fact, the abbreviation "pseud." may appear in brackets after the name.

If the work is that of two or three authors, all the names are set down in normal order. If there are more than three authors, it is usual to give only the name of the first author mentioned on the title page and to follow it with "*et al.*" (and others). (See example *d*, p. 32.)

Some works are compilations, and as such the name of a compiler or editor is given in the place of the author (see example *h*, p. 32).

The "author" may be the name of a corporate body—a country, state, city, legislative body, institution, society, business firm (see example *r*, p. 34).

(2) *Title of the work.*—Enter the title of a book as it appears on the title page; enter the title of an article in a periodical as it appears at the head of the article. In both cases follow the peculiarities of spelling and the punctuation within the title, but capitalize in conformance with the scheme adopted for the paper as a whole (see sec. 28, p. 29).

Underline the title of a whole published work, that is, underline the title of a book and of a periodical; "quote" (i.e., place between quotation marks) the title of an article in a periodical. Put a comma after the title of a book unless it is followed immediately by a parenthesis enclosing the facts of publication, in which case put the comma after the final parenthesis. Put a comma between the title of an article and the title of a periodical (being careful to place the comma inside the second quotation mark), and put a comma after the title of a periodical.

Since display headings, both on title pages and at the heads of articles, frequently set a title in two or more lines and since punctuation is commonly omitted at the ends of display headings, it frequently is necessary to add marks of punctuation to a title. This occurs most often in titles composed of a main title and a subtitle. In the following, for example, *The Law and the Working of the Constitution: Documents, 1660–1914*, the subtitle, *Documents, 1660–1914*, appeared on a separate line and there was no punctuation after *Constitution*. Copied without change from the title page, the title is:

Wrong: The Law and Working of the Constitution Documents, 1660-1914.

Adding a colon after *Constitution* clarifies the meaning.

Right: The Law and Working of the Constitution: Documents, 1660-1914.

(3) *Name of editor, compiler, and/or translator.* Enter the name as it appears on the title page and place before it "ed.," "comp.," or "trans." as may be appropriate. Placed before the name, these abbreviations stand respectively for "edited by," "compiled by," "translated by."

The Works of Shakespear, ed. Alexander Pope (6 vols.; London: Printed for Jacob Tonson in the Strand, 1723-25), II, 38.

It should be noted, however, that in a paper dealing with the works of Alexander Pope, Pope's name would precede the title *The Works of Shakespear*, the note being set up in the following form:

(4) *Facts of publication.* As listed under (4) on page 20 they are:

    (*a*) *Number of volumes.* This is not necessary except in a note referring to a work as a whole. If included, write, e.g., "4 vols.," not "vols. 4" or "IV vols.," and add a semicolon.

    (*b*) *Number of the edition.* Write, e.g., "1st ed. rev." or "2d ed.," followed by a semicolon.

    (*c*) *Series title.* Capitalize to accord with the scheme chosen for listing titles of books, articles, periodicals, etc. (see sec. 28, p. 29), enclose the title in quotation marks, and follow with a semicolon.

Exception: If it is necessary to list two or more of the foregoing "facts," separate with commas, reserving the semicolon to follow the last item.

    (*d*) *Place of publication.* When the names of several cities appear under the publisher's imprint, the city first mentioned is assumed to be the location of the editorial offices, and this is the one to list. Follow with a colon. If the city is one whose location is not commonly known, give both city and state, separating the two with a comma and placing the colon after the state.

    (*e*) *Name of publishing agency.* Copy this in exactly the form given on the title page, unless a consistent use of shortened forms, as listed in the *Cumulative Book Index*, is adopted. Follow with a comma.

    (*f*) *Date of publication.* If no date appears on the title page, list the copyright date. If no copyright date is shown, write "n.d." (for "no date") in place of the date. If the date of publication has been established by another means, however, enclose the date in brackets.

For a work of more than one volume published over a period of more than a year, give the inclusive dates of publication, e.g., "1935–1940."

If publication of the work is still in progress, indicate this fact by placing a dash after the first date, e.g., "1935—."

As indicated earlier (see sec. 22, *a*, 4, p. 20), all the facts of publication are grouped together and placed between parentheses. Frequently, only two items of information are given, and in all such cases they are separated with a comma. In some fields it is common practice to omit the name of the publisher. If this is done, the facts of publication might read, e.g., "(2d ed.; New York, 1950)," or some other variant form giving total number of volumes or series title, or, if none of these is necessary, simply "(New York, 1950)."

For most periodical references it is not necessary to give the facts of publication other than the date, and, since this is related closely to the volume number, it is treated in section (5) below.

(5) *Volume number*. If the book is in more than one volume, the footnote must mention the volume number. Write the number in Roman numerals. If the volumes were published in different years, the footnote must indicate this fact either by giving inclusive dates of publication and placing the volume number after the facts of publication, as:

John Grote, <u>History of Greece</u> (New York: Harper & Bros., 1853-72), V, 249.

or by giving only the publication date of the specific volume referred to and placing the volume number before the facts of publication:

> John Grote, <u>History of Greece</u>, V (New York: Harper & Bros., 1860), 249.

If all the volumes were published in the same year, the volume number may either precede or follow the facts of publication; but there is the advantage in putting it after the facts of publication of indicating to the reader that the entire work, not just the volume mentioned in the note, was published in the year mentioned.

> William C. Costin and John S. Watson, <u>The Law and Working of the Constitution: Documents, 1660-1914</u> (New York: Macmillan Co., 1952), II, 321.

In references to periodicals, write the volume number after the name of the periodical, using capital Roman numerals regardless of whether the periodical named uses Roman or Arabic numerals. Put the date—month and year—after the volume number; separate them with a comma and place between parentheses, putting a comma after the final parenthesis. It is permissible to omit the month if the number of the issue follows the volume number, e.g., "Vol. XX, No. 12 (1950)," instead of "Vol. XX (Dec., 1950)." If it is known that the periodical has used but one series of volume numbers since it began publication, both month and date may be omitted, although their inclusion is a convenience.

It is not necessary to give the volume number of a daily, weekly, or semimonthly publication; month, day, and year identify them most readily:

> "A Letter from the Publisher," <u>Time</u>, June 14, 1954, p. 54.

(6) *Page number*. Refer to a single page as, e.g., "p. 60." But refer to more than one page as, e.g., "pp. 60–61," not "pp. 60–1." Similarly, write "pp. 140–42," not "pp. 140–2." If the first number ends in two ciphers, write, e.g., "pp. 400–402," not "pp. 400–02" or "pp. 400–2." If the first digit in the second number is higher than that in the first number, write both numbers in full, e.g., "pp. 295–315," not "pp. 295–15."

The citation of exact page references is preferable to the use of, say, "pp. 60f." (page 60 and following page) and "pp. 140ff." (page 140 and following pages).

23. *Parts that should be designated by Roman numerals.*—It will be noticed in the examples that capital Roman numerals are used to express volume numbers, and Arabic numerals to express page numbers. This is general practice except in scientific papers. Roman numerals (capitals) are commonly used also for references to Part, Division, Act, except for references to classical and other ancient works (see sec. 42, p. 41). Roman numerals (lower-case, e.g., i, ii, v, ix, etc.) should be used for references to chapters, to introductory pages in a book (preface, etc.), to scenes in a play, and to books in classical works.

24. *Parts that should be designated by Arabic numerals.*—Arabic numerals should be used for references to pages and lines and for all divisions of classical works except books.

25. *Omission of abbreviations for "Vol." and "p."*—In a reference including *both* a volume and a page number, it is permissible to omit the abbreviations "Vol." and "p." or "pp."

W. T. Jones, A History of Western Philosophy (New York: Harcourt, Brace & Co., 1952), II, 940.

But, if in addition to volume and page some other division is mentioned, that division must be appropriately designated, as, for example:

> Gröber, Grundriss der romanischen Philologie (Strassburg, 1889-97), II, Part II, 5.

In certain kinds of references omission of "Vol." and "p." might result in ambiguity. In the following, for example, the volume number is that of the series rather than of the specific work:

> R. H. Fletcher, Arthurian Material in the Chronicles ("Harvard Studies and Notes in Philology and Literature," Vol. X; Boston, 1906), pp. 145-46.

And in the following, the relationship of the two titles is clearer when the volume number is designated as such:

> T. C. Chamberlin and R. D. Salisbury, Geology, Vol. I: Geologic Processes and Their Results (2d ed. rev.; New York: Henry Holt & Co., 1906), p. 155.

26. *Titles that should be underlined and those that should be "quoted."* —In general, titles of written works, published or unpublished, are either underlined or "quoted" (i.e., placed between double quotation marks), depending upon their form.

The general rule is to underline the titles of *whole published works* (which in printed matter are italicized) and to quote the titles of *component parts* and of *unpublished materials*. This scheme should be followed wherever the titles appear in the paper.

a) Underline the titles of all the following kinds of published materials: books, pamphlets, bulletins, periodicals (magazines and journals), newspapers, yearbooks, plays, motion pictures, symphonies and operas, as well as poems, essays, lectures, sermons, proceedings, and reports appearing as separate publications. If the separate volumes of a work have titles, underline these titles as well as the title of the whole work (see example *l*, p. 33).

    b) *Quote* the titles of chapters or other divisions of books; subdivisions of whole publications, such as articles in periodicals; essays, poems, lectures, sermons, etc., published as part of a collection; series titles, radio and television programs, short musical compositions; and unpublished works, such as typed or "processed" reports, lectures, minutes, theses. But note that when a processed work (lithoprinted, multilithed, multigraphed, etc.) appearing as a separate publication bears a publisher's imprint, the title should be underlined.

27. *Titles that should be neither underlined nor "quoted."*—The names of the books of the Bible and of all sacred scriptures (Koran, Upanishads, Vedanta, etc.) are neither underlined nor quoted.

28. *Capitalization of titles.*—Two methods of capitalization of titles of English works are recognized; but one scheme or the other should be adopted and used consistently throughout the paper, both in the footnote and the bibliographical entries and wherever else the titles appear. The two schemes are:

    a) Capitalization of the first and last words, nouns, pronouns, adjectives, adverbs, and verbs.

    b) Capitalization of the first word, proper nouns, and proper adjectives.

    In the titles of French, Italian, and Spanish works, the first word, all proper nouns, but not the adjectives derived from proper nouns, are capitalized.

    In the titles of German works, the first word and all nouns and words used as nouns are capitalized. Of the adjectives derived from nouns, only those derived from the names of persons are capitalized.

An exception to the schemes of capitalization here mentioned may be made in a paper concerned, for example, with a specific edition of a work, or with a manuscript, when the exact manner in which the title appeared is significant.

29. *Omission of author's name, or of name and title, in footnotes.*—If at the first mention of a work the author's full name is brought into the text close to the footnote number, it may be omitted in the note. After the first reference, mention in the text of the surname alone permits its omission in the note.

Similarly, if both name and title of the work are given in the text, they may be omitted in the note, which then might consist either of the facts of publication and volume and/or page, or of the reference alone.

30. *Abbreviations.*—In footnote and bibliographical materials, a word designating a part of a work may be abbreviated if it is followed by a number. In the list of standard abbreviations below, note that those underlined should always be underlined; that the kind of numeral (Roman—capital or small—or Arabic) following a part should be the kind used in designating that part; that an abbreviation here capitalized should always be capitalized, but that the others should be capitalized only when they begin a footnote.

```
art. iv (plural, arts.), article
Bk. I (plural, Bks.; in classical references small Roman numerals
    are used, e.g., Bk. i), book
c. 220 (plural, cc. [used in law citations only]), chapter
ca., about
cf., compare
chap. ii (plural, chaps.), chapter
col. 6 (plural, cols.), column
2d ed. (plural, edd.), edition
ed. (plural, eds.), editor ("ed." [i.e., the singular form] may
    also be used for "edited by")
et al. (et alii), "and others"
Fig. 2 (plural, Figs.), figure
infra, below
l. 10 (plural, ll.), line
```

```
MS (plural, MSS), manuscript
n. 5 (plural, nn.), note, footnote
n.d., no date
n.n., no name
n.p., no place
No. 12 (plural, Nos.), number
p. (plural, pp.), page
par. (plural, pars.), paragraph
passim, here and there (frequently preceded by et, "and")
Pt. (plural, Pts.), part
sec. 9 (plural, secs.), section
supra, above
trans., translator, translated by
vs. 4 (plural, vss.), verse
Vol. II (plural, Vols.), volume
```

Titles of well-known journals, publications of learned societies, and dictionaries may be abbreviated in capital letters, without spaces or periods, for use in footnotes but not in bibliographical entries.

```
MLN, Modern Language Notes
PMLA, Publications of the Modern Language Association
HDB, Hastings' Dictionary of the Bible
OED, Oxford English Dictionary
```

Also, it is permissible for the writer who must refer frequently to the same work to devise an abbreviation to be used after the first, full reference.

Basic Forms: Books, Reports, Articles

31. The following examples illustrate correct forms for use in all papers except those in scientific fields (see chap. vii).

a) One author:

[1]Daniel Aaron, Men of Good Hope: A Story of American Progressives (New York: Oxford University Press, 1951), p. 38.

b) Two authors:

[2]Ruth I. Baldwin and John R. Clark, Arithmetic for Young America (Yonkers-on-Hudson, N.Y.: World Book Co., 1944), p. 11.

c) *Three authors:*

[3]Joseph P. Chamberlain, Noel T. Dowling, and Paul R. Hayes, The Judicial Function in Federal Administrative Agencies (New York: Commonwealth Fund, 1942), p. 97.

d) *More than three authors:*

[4]G. M. Dutcher et al. [or G. M. Dutcher and Others], Guide to Historical Literature (New York: Macmillan Co., 1931), p. 50.

e) *No author given:*

[5]The Lottery (London: J. Watts, [1732]), pp. 20-25.

[An alternate method uses "Anon." before the title.]

f) *No author given; name supplied:*

[6][Henry Z. Blank], "Art for Its Own Sake," Magazine of New Art, XXX (January, 1912), 85-90.

g) *Pseudonymous author; real name supplied:*

[7]Helen Delay [Willa Cather], "Out of Their Pulpits," The Library, I, No. 6 (April 14, 1900), 20.

h) *Editor of a collection:*

[8]J. N. D. Anderson (ed.), The World's Religions (London: Inter-Varsity Fellowship, 1950), p. 143.

i) *Translator of original work [same form used for editor of an original work]:*

[9]Karl Barth, The Doctrine of the Word of God, trans. G. T. Thompson (New York: Charles Scribner's Sons, 1936), p. 80.

j) *Edition:*

[10]Sir Alan Gardiner, Egyptian Grammar (2d ed. rev.; London: Oxford University Press, 1950), p. 250.

k) Series—book and monograph:

[11]G. K. Chesterton, Robert Browning ("English Men of Letters"; New York: Macmillan Co., 1910), p. 56.

[12]Virgil K. Whittaker, The Religious Basis of Spenser's Thought ("Stanford University Publications: Language and Literature," Vol. VII, No. 3; Stanford, Calif.: Stanford University Press, 1950), p. 36.

l) Work of several volumes under one general title, with each volume under a separate title:

[13]T. C. Chamberlin and R. D. Salisbury, Geology, Vol. I: Geologic Processes and Their Results (2d ed. rev.; New York: Henry Holt & Co., 1906), p. 155.

m) Work of several volumes under one title and edited by one person, with each volume under a separate title and by a different author:

[14]J. H. Latané, America as a World Power, 1897-1907, Vol. XXV of The American Nation: A History, ed. A. B. Hart (28 vols.; New York: Harper & Bros., 1904-18), p. 220.

n) Component part by one author in a collection edited by others:

[15]Archibald MacMechan, "Thoreau," Cambridge History of American Literature, ed. William P. Trent, John Erskine, Stuart P. Sherman, and Carl Van Doren (New York: Macmillan Co., 1931), II, Part II, 12.

o) Privately printed work:

[16]Marcel J. DeMeirleir, Manufactural Occupance in the West Central Area of Chicago, Department of Geography Research Paper No. 11, University of Chicago (Chicago: By the author, 1950), p. 11.

p) Report—no author given:

[17]Annual Report of the Board of Regents of the Smithsonian Institution for the Year Ending June 30, 1932 (Washington: U.S. Government Printing Office, 1933), p. 20.

q) Report—author given:

[18]James W. Angell, Financial Foreign Policy of the United States, A Report to the Second International Studies Conference on the State and Economic Life, London, May 29 to June 2, 1933, Prepared by the American Committee Appointed by the Council on Foreign Relations (New York: The Conference, 1933), pp. 5-7.

r) Report—association the author:

[19]American Medical Association, Medical Relations under Workmen's Compensation, A Report Prepared by the Bureau of Medical Economics (Chicago: American Medical Association, 1933), p. 3.

s) Article in a yearbook:

[20]G. M. Wilson, "A Survey of the Social and Business Use of Arithmetic," Second Report of the Committee on Minimal Essentials in Elementary-School Subjects, Sixteenth Yearbook of the National Society for the Study of Education, Part I (Bloomington, Ill.: Public School Publishing Co., 1917), pp. 20-22.

t) Proceedings:

[21]Industrial Relations Research Association, Proceedings of Third Annual Meeting (Madison, Wis., 1951), pp. 140-83.

u) Article in a journal—author given:

[22]L. A. Weissberger, "Macchiavelli and Tudor England," Journal of Political Economy, XLII (February, 1927), 589.

v) Article in a periodical—no author given:

[23]"Schooling for a Speaker," Time, June 14, 1954, p. 54.

w) Book review:

[24]Henry D. Aiken, Review of The Moral Nature of Man, by A. Campbell Garnett, Ethics, LXIII (January, 1953), 140-42.

x) Signed article in an encyclopaedia—editor's name given:

[25]E. E. Kellett, "Spinoza," Encyclopedia of Religion and Ethics, ed. James Hastings, XI (1921), 251.

[26]"Electricity," <u>Encyclopaedia Britannica</u>, 14th ed., Vol. VIII.

[Not necessary to give names of the many editors of an encyclopaedia such as the <u>Britannica</u>.]

Special Forms: Public Documents

32. *Form of citations.*—The form used for citing public documents should be one that makes them readily accessible to anyone wishing to locate them in a library. The arrangement of information on the title pages of the documents themselves, its amount and complexity, raise puzzling questions of how much of the information it is necessary to include and in what order it should be set down in the footnote. Here reference to the card catalogue of the library can be of great help, although it is not a safe guide in such matters as capitalization and punctuation, which for public documents as well as other references must follow the scheme of the paper. When in doubt of how much to include in a reference, it is better to err on the side of giving too much rather than too little information.

The name of the country, state, city, town, or other government district (e.g., U.S., Great Britain, Illinois, Baltimore) is given first in the citation of an official publication issued by one of them or under its auspices. Then comes the name of the legislative body, court, executive department, bureau, board, commission, or committee. The name of the office rather than the title of the officer should be given except where the title of the officer is the only name of the office, as, e.g., "Illinois, State Entomologist." The name of the division, regional office, etc., if any, follows the name of the department, bureau, or commission. Thus the "author" of a document might read: "U.S., Bureau of Foreign and Domestic Commerce, Office of International Trade." Ordinarily, the title of the document, if it has a title, comes next. From this point, the information varies with the document. The following examples should aid in devising suitable forms for similar materials.

33. *Examples, U.S. documents:*

[1]U.S., Statutes at Large, XXIV, Part 1, 866.

[2]U.S., Congress, An Act To Increase the Borrowing Power of the Commodity Credit Corporation, Public Law 579, 81st Cong., 2d Sess., 1950, p. 2.

[3]U.S., Congress, Senate, Progress on Hoover Commission Recommendations, 81st Cong., 1st Sess., 1949, Rept. 1158, p. 4.

[4]U.S., Congress, House, Committee on Interstate and Foreign Commerce, National Foundation Act of 1949, 81st Cong., 1st Sess., 1949, H. Rept. 796 to accompany H.R. 4846, p. 9.

[5]U.S., Congress, House, To Prevent Profiteering in War Munitions, 76th Cong., 2d Sess., 1940, H.R. 7545, p. 1.

[6]U.S., Congress, House, Committee on Labor, Minority Report, Proposed Amendments to the National Labor Relations Act, Report No. 1928, Part 3, 76th Cong., 3d Sess., 1940, p. 10.

[7]U.S., Congress, House, Committee on Banking and Currency, Hearings, Defense Housing and Community Facilities, 82d Cong., 1st Sess., 1951, pp. 82-83.

[8]U.S., Congress, Senate, Committee on Labor and Public Welfare, Hearings, on S. 249, Labor Relations, 81st Cong., 1st Sess., 1949, p. 12.

[9]U.S., Congress, Senate, Subcommittee of the Committee on the Judiciary, Hearings, Investigation of the National Labor Relations Board, 75th Cong., 3d Sess., 1938, p. 3.

[10]U.S., Congressional Record, 80th Cong., 2d Sess., 1948, XCIV, Part 8, 9553.

[11]Printing Law of 1895, in U.S., Statutes at Large, XXVIII, 601-24.

[12]U.S., Bureau of Labor Statistics, Monthly Labor Review, LXIV (1947), 765.

[13]U.S., Bureau of the Census, Fifteenth Census of the United States: 1930. Population, II, 98.

[14]Commonwealth of Massachusetts, Report of the Governor's Labor-Management Committee, House of Representatives No. 1875, March 13, 1947.

[15]U.S., Congress, House, Alaska: A Reconnaissance Report on the Potential Water Resources . . . , 82d Cong., 1st Sess., 1952, House Doc. 197, p. 92.

[16]U.S., President, 1945-53 (Truman), The National Emergency; Address and Proclamation, Washington, D.C., Dec. 15 and 16, 1950, Department of State Publication No. 4052 (Washington: U.S. Government Printing Office, 1950), pp. 12-13.

34. *Public documents bearing names of personal authors:*

[17]H. R. Hockmuth, Earl R. Franklin, and Marion Clawson, Sheep Migration in the Intermountain Region, U.S. Dept. of Agriculture Circular No. 624 (Washington: U.S. Government Printing Office, 1942), p. 24.

[18]Samuel Flagg Bemis and Grace Gardner Griffin, Guide to the Diplomatic History of the United States, 1775-1921 (Washington: U.S. Government Printing Office, 1953), p. 167.

[19]Illinois, Department of Public Welfare, The Illinois Plan of Fiscal Control in the Division of Old-Age Assistance, by John C. Weigel and Fletcher C. Kettle (Springfield, 1939), p. 32.

[20]U.S., Bureau of Labor Statistics, in co-operation with the American Library Association, Economic Status of Library Personnel, 1949, prepared by Lily Mary David (Chicago: American Library Association, 1950), p. 48.

35. *Examples, British documents:*

[21]Great Britain, 3 Hansard's Parliamentary Debates, XXX (1835), 452.

[22]Great Britain, 5 Parliamentary Debates (Commons), LXXVI (1915), 1723. [Since 1909 the Debates have been published separately for the two houses of Parliament. The name "Hansard" is properly omitted from the title after 1891, although it still has official sanction and is often used.]

[23]Great Britain, Parliamentary Papers, Vol. XIX (Accounts and Papers, Vol. VII), Cmd. 3157, July, 1928, "Government Grants to Local Authorities," p. 69.

[The Parliamentary Papers, bound annually in consecutive volumes of Bills, Reports, and Accounts and Papers. Note that while the Parliamentary Papers have their own volume numbers, each volume is a different volume number either of Bills, Reports, or Accounts and Papers. These in turn are composed of "command papers," each with a separate number and title.]

[24]Great Britain, Public Record Office, Calendar of State Papers, Colonial Series, America and the West Indies, 1733 (London: His Majesty's Stationery Office, 1939), p. 223.

[25]Great Britain, Public Record Office, Calendar of State Papers Relating to Scotland and Mary, Queen of Scots, 1547-1603, VIII (1585-86), 128.

[26]Great Britain, Ministry of Health, Parliamentary Papers, Vol. XIX (Accounts and Papers, Vol. VII), Cmd. 3134, "Proposals for Reform in Local Government and in the Financial Relations between the Exchequer and the Local Authorities," p. 24.

[27]Great Britain, Sovereigns, etc., 1558-1603 (Elizabeth), A Proclamation for the Observation of Certain Statutes, with a Fourme How the Same Shall Be Executed: . . . (London: R. Jugge and J. Cawood, 1562), p. 45.

36. *Examples, French documents.*—The French *Débats parlementaires* and the *Documents* are each published in a separate series for the Chamber of Deputies and the Senate. Since the volume numbers do not begin with each year, it is important that the date as well as the volume number be given:

[28]France, Annales de la chambre des députés, Débats parlementaires, LVII (1899), Part II, 132.

[29]France, Annales du sénat, Documents, LXI (1902), 843.

[30]France, Ministère des Affaires Étrangères, Documents diplomatiques français, 1871-1914, 1re série, IX (Paris: Imprimerie nationale, 1939), 665.

37. *Examples, League of Nations and United Nations documents:*

[31]League of Nations, Secretariat, Application of Part II of the Opium Convention (O.C. 114) (Geneva, 1923), p. 5.

[32]United Nations, Economic and Social Council, Commission on Human Rights, Study of the Legal Validity of the Undertakings concerning Minorities (E/CN.4/367, Apr. 7, 1950) (Lake Success, 1950), p. 16.

The name of the organization, with the document number, date, and page, would be a satisfactory form to use after the first citation. A paper making many references to such documents, particularly if it was designed for readers familiar with these or similar documents, might use the abbreviated form at all times.

Special Forms: Legal Citations

38. *Form of citation.*—Federal and state constitutions, state laws, and the like are referred to by article, section, and chapter (abbreviated "c." in legal citations). British statutes ordinarily cite the regnal year of the sovereign, and the references should include it. The title of the statute may be included or not, as the discussion may seem to require (see nn. 39, 40).

In citing legal cases, the title of the case is underlined. When the title consists of names of plaintiff and defendant, the "v." for "versus" is not underlined. The volume number precedes the abbreviated title of the report, and page number and date follow (see n. 41). Since court decisions usually appear in two or more reports, the reference frequently mentions more than one report; the official report is cited first (see n. 42). Some federal and state reports are known by the name of the official reporter. For a reporter of the U.S. Supreme Court, "U.S." should appear after the name; for a state reporter, the state abbreviation (see nn. 43, 44).

The decisions of various governmental agencies are cited in the same general form as court decisions (see n. 45).

39. *Examples of legal citations:*

[33]U.S., Constitution, Art. 4, sec. 3.

[34]Illinois, Constitution (1848), Art. 5, sec. 2.
[The date of a Constitution is indicated ordinarily only when it is not the one in force.]

[35]Illinois, Revised Statutes (1949), c. 20, sec. 4.

[36]California, Civil Code (1949), secs. 1040-46.

[37]Kentucky, Revised Statutes, Annotated (Baldwin, 1943), sec. 381.040.
[This refers to an annotated revision of these statutes made by William E. Baldwin in 1943.]

[38]Massachusetts, Annotated Laws (Supplement, 1951), c. 184, sec. 8.

[39]Great Britain, Statutes at Large, 3 and 4 Geo. VI, c. 1 (1944).

[40]Great Britain, Statutes at Large, 12 and 13 Geo. VI, c. 51 (1949), "Legal Aid and Advice Act."

[41]Lisenba v. State of California, 314 U.S. 219 (1939).

[42]Crocker v. Cotting, 173 Mass. 68, 53 N.E. 158 (1899).

[43]Collector v. Day, 11 Wallace (U.S.), 113 (1870).

[44]Rice v. Boston & Worcester R.R. Co., 12 Allen (Mass.), 141 (1866).

[45]International Shoe Co., 93 N.L.R.B. 907 (1951).

Other Special Forms

40. *Newspapers:*

[27]Chicago Tribune, March 17, 1954, p. 14. [Name of city underlined because it is part of the title. Ordinarily page number should be given when reference is to a large paper.]

[28]The Times (London), May 1, 1949, p. 8. ["London" is not a part of the title in this case, but it must be mentioned to distinguish which Times is meant.]

41. *Scriptural references.*—The names of the books of the Bible, of the Apocrypha, of the Apocalyptic, and of versions of the Bible should be abbreviated when exact references are given (see *A Manual of Style* [11th rev. ed.], pp. 68–69, for a list of abbreviations). The names are not underlined.

[29]Isa. 12:5.

[30]I Cor. 13:12.

42. *Classical references.*—Books are indicated with small Roman numerals; the remaining divisions, with Arabic numerals (see nn. 31, 32 below). For classical works not divided into books, all the divisions are indicated with Arabic numerals (see nn. 33, 34). Use no punctuation between author's name and title of the work, and none after the title; separate the various divisions of the work with periods except when a succession of lines, sections, pages is to be indicated (nn. 31, 32).

[31]Cicero Tusculanae disputationes ii. 2. 22. 52, 54.

[32]Quintilian Inst. xi. 3. 58, 60. [The titles of some classical works are commonly abbreviated.]

[33]Aristotle Poetics 20. 1456[b] 20. 34-35.

[34]Plutarch Pericles 10. 1.

43. *Unpublished materials.*—These are of various sorts, and it is not possible to give here examples of all. If the material appears under a title, this title is "quoted" (i.e., placed between quotation marks; see nn. 41–44 below). If the writer of the paper supplies a title, or adds to an original title whose form without the addition would not identify the material, such title is not "quoted" (see nn. 39, 40 below).

a) *Manuscript collections.*—The location, title, and number, or similar designation should be given. If a specific document or letter is referred to, it should be mentioned either at the beginning or at the end of the note.

[35]British Museum, Harleian MSS, 5105, fol. 37.

[36]Petition of Briggs, Feb. 8, 1806, Public Record Office MSS, Foreign Office, Egypt, Vol. II.

[37]Decimal files, Department of State, Washington, 741.9411/76, Wright to Long, Apr. 29, 1921.

b) Letters, reports, minutes, etc., in private files.—References
to such materials may give much or little information,
depending upon their significance in the discussion. Thus
reference to a letter might be "John Blank, personal letter,"
or in another case a reference might give, not only the name
of the writer of the letter, but his official position, and the
place and date as well.

[38] Letter from Hon. T. E. Murphy, Secretary, State of
Rhode Island and Providence Plantations State Public Welfare Commission, Providence, R.I., June 21, 1933.

[39] Final Report to the Chairman of the English Department
by the Committee Appointed To Study the Undergraduate Curriculum,
Everyman's College, November 10, 1940 (in the files of the Department).

[40] Minutes of the Annual Meeting, June 5, 1893, Society
for the Betterment of Working Conditions of Domestic Help, New
World City, Mass. (in the files of the Society).

[41] "Survey of the Immediate Relief Situation in Illinois,
Prepared by the American Association of Social Workers" (School
of Social Service Administration, University of Chicago, July,
1936), p. 6. (Mimeographed.)

[42] Ethel Miles, "Girls' Reading Interests," Paper read before the meeting of the Scarsdale Library Club, Scarsdale, New
York, March 26, 1937.

c) Theses and dissertations:

[43] Helen Margaret Reynolds, "University Library Buildings
in the United States, 1890-1939" (unpublished Master's dissertation, Library School, University of Illinois, 1946), p. 48.

[44] Mary Catherine Welborn, "Calendar Reform in the Thir-
teenth Century" (unpublished Ph.D. dissertation, Dept. of History, University of Chicago), p. 80.

44. *Interviews.*—Although not a written source, personal interviews
are much relied upon in some pieces of research and will require
mention in the footnotes. References to them follow the same
general pattern as that used for letters:

[45] Interview with the Director of Promotion, May 4, 1954.

[46] Interview with John Springer, Pres. CIO, UAW Local 889, Apr. 9, 1954.

45. *Citation taken from a secondary source.*—If the source consulted is secondary, this fact must be indicated in the reference. The choice of forms should be determined by the requirements in the individual case. For example, in the following reference if the important fact with regard to the statement is that the authority for it occurs in the *Jesuit Relations*, the first form is preferable; but if, on the other hand, it is Hulbert's citation of it that is significant, the second form should be used.

[47] Jesuit Relations and Allied Documents, Vol. LIX, n. 41, quoted in [or "cited by"] Archer Butler Hulbert, Portage Paths (Cleveland: Arthur H. Clark, 1903), p. 181.

Or the reverse form:

[48] Archer Butler Hulbert, Portage Paths (Cleveland: Arthur H. Clark, 1903), p. 181, quoting [or "citing"] Jesuit Relations and Allied Documents, Vol. LIX, n. 41.

SECOND OR LATER REFERENCES

When a work has once been cited in complete form, later references to it should be in shortened form.

46. *When "ibid." is to be used.*—When references to the same work follow each other without any intervening reference, even though separated by several pages, the abbreviation *ibid.* (for the Latin *ibidem*, "in the same place") is used to repeat as much of the preceding reference as is appropriate for the new entry:

[1] Wilbur L. Cross, The History of Henry Fielding (2d ed.; New Haven: Yale University Press, 1918), I, 49. [A first, and therefore complete, reference to the work.]

[2] Ibid. [With no intervening reference, a second reference to the same volume and page of Cross's work requires only ibid.]

[3] Ibid., II, 51. [Here another volume and page number of Cross's work are referred to.]

Ibid. may also be used to repeat the title of a journal in the immediately preceding reference if the author is the same; the title of the article may be different.

[4]Sune V. Main, "Matthew 10: An Interpretation," Journal of the New Testament, XXXVII (June, 1918), 37.

[5]Sune V. Main, "The First Epistle to the Corinthians," ibid., XXXIX (June, 1920), 84.

If a number of pages separate the references to a given work, the writer may prefer, for the sake of clarity, to repeat the title rather than to use *ibid.* even though no reference to another work has intervened.

Since *ibid.* means "in the same *place*," it must not be employed to repeat the author's name alone when this is the only item remaining unchanged from the footnote immediately preceding. In such cases the repetition of the author's name is preferred style, although *idem* (meaning "the same") may be used. *Idem* should not be abbreviated to *id*.

Wrong:

[1]Arthur Waley, The Analects of Confucius (London: George Allen & Unwin, 1938), p. 33.

[2]Ibid., Chinese Poems (London: George Allen & Unwin, 1946), p. 51.

Right:

[1]Arthur Waley, The Analects of Confucius (London: George Allen & Unwin, 1938), p. 33.

[2]Arthur Waley, Chinese Poems (London: George Allen & Unwin, 1946), p. 51.

47. *When "ibid." is not to be used.*—Reference to a work which already has been cited in full form, *but not in the reference immediately preceding*, should be made in one of the two ways outlined in the following. The methods must not be interchanged in the same piece of work; that is, if Method A is chosen, neither *op. cit.* nor *loc. cit.* may appear in the footnotes at any time. But if two or more works by the same author have been cited, repetition of the title—in shortened form if desired—is required under both methods. (Use of *loc. cit.* under Method B is an exception to this rule. See 2, *a* and *b*, p. 47).

a) Method A.—This is the simpler method, and one that appears to be growing in favor. For reference to a book, the author's surname (not forename or initials unless another author of the same surname has been cited), with volume and/or page number is given. If more than one work by the same author has been referred to, subsequent references to the works of that author must mention the title—in shortened form, if desired. Mention of works issued anonymously and of works by corporate bodies likewise call for the titles. Reference to a magazine article repeats the name of the magazine but may omit the title of the article.

The following group of footnotes is illustrative:

[1] G. D. H. Cole, A Short History of the British Working Class Movement (New York: Macmillan Co., 1927), III, 125.

[2] Robert A. Dahl, "Workers' Control of Industry and the British Labour Party," American Political Science Review, XLI, No. 5 (October, 1947), 890-93.

[3] Cole, III, 148. [Refers again to Cole's book, cited in full form in n. 1.]

[4] G. D. H. Cole, Self-Government in Industry (5th ed. rev.; London: G. Bell & Co., Ltd., 1920), p. 42. [Here a second book by Cole is introduced.]

[5] Dahl, American Political Science Review, XLI, No. 5, 895. [Another reference to Dahl's article. Since it has been cited earlier in complete form, the title of the article may be omitted. One sometimes sees the title of the article given and the title of the journal omitted. This is poor documentation, since the volume number refers to the journal, not the article.]

[6] Letter of Charles Evans Hughes to William E. Borah, July 6, 1921, in William E. Borah Papers (Library of Congress, Washington, D.C.), Box 630. Cited hereafter as Borah Papers. [A first reference to a collection, which includes a notation of the way in which the collection will be referred to in later references.]

[7] U.S. Senate, Committee on Education and Labor, Hearings, National Labor Relations Board, 74th Cong. 1st Sess., 1935, p. 520. Cited hereafter as Senate Committee on Education and Labor, NLRB Hearings, 1935. [First reference to these Hearings.]

[8] Cole, A Short History . . . , II, 50. [Refers again to one of the two books by Cole cited earlier in full. The author's name with title in shortened form is used. The author's name with volume and page number, as in n. 3, would not identify the book, since at this point two of his books have been mentioned.]

[9] Senate Committee on Education and Labor, NLRB Hearings, 1935, p. 811. [Another reference to the Hearings first mentioned in n. 7. The form here given is preferred style, although it is permissible to omit the title, as would be done if the author were a person.]

[10] Hughes to Borah, July 6, 1921, Borah Papers, Box 630. [Another reference to the letter referred to in n. 6, using the shortened form of reference to the collection there set forth.]

If the author's name is brought into the text, it may be omitted in the shortened form of reference the same as in the full form. (See p. 45.)

b) *Method B.*—This method uses the author's surname (but not forename or initials unless another author of the same surname has been cited), followed by either *op. cit.* (for the Latin *opere citato,* "in the work cited") or by *loc. cit.* (for the Latin *loco citato,* "in the place cited"), such as may be suitable according to the usages here defined.

(1) *Op. cit.* is used to refer to a work previously cited in full form when a *different part* (volume and/or page, chapter, or the like) is cited and when *ibid.* may not be used because references to other works have intervened. Thus *op. cit.* is normally followed by a specific reference,

although it may appear alone with the author's name if the work in general rather than a particular part is referred to.

(2) *Loc. cit.* is used under two different conditions:

(*a*) To repeat the same reference to a book (same volume and/or page) as that last cited when references to other works have intervened. In such cases the author's name with *loc. cit.* is all that the footnote contains. It will be seen that the author's name and *op. cit. plus* notation of the volume and/or page number would be equally correct (provided, of course, that only one work by the author has been mentioned), and this form should be used in preference to *loc. cit.* if a number of pages have intervened, and especially if several other notes have intervened.

(*b*) To make subsequent reference to a magazine article or other component part of a larger work, or to a document in a collection. To indicate that such references are "in the *place* cited" conveys a more accurate idea than to say that they are "in the *work* cited." For use in this connection, *loc. cit.* is frequently followed by a notation of volume, page, box, file, or the like.

The following group of footnotes illustrates the correct use of *loc. cit.*:

[1]G. D. H. Cole, <u>A Short History of the British Working Class Movement</u> (New York: Macmillan Co., 1927), III, 125.

[2]G. D. H. Cole, <u>Self-Government in Industry</u> (5th ed. rev.; London: G. Bell & Co., Ltd., 1920), p. 42.

[3]Robert A. Dahl, "Workers' Control of Industry and the British Labour Party," <u>American Political Science Review</u>, XLI, No. 5 (October, 1947), 890-93.

[4]Ibid., p. 891. [Refers to Dahl's article. Since no reference intervenes between the first and the succeeding citation of the article, ibid. rather than loc. cit. is proper. Note that whereas "Vol." and "p." were omitted in the preceding reference, the "p." is required in note 4, where ibid. covers the volume number.]

[5]Cole, loc. cit. [Refers to the work by Cole last mentioned, same page as in that reference.]

[6]Dahl, loc. cit. [Refers to p. 891 of Dahl's article.]

[7]Letter of Charles Evans Hughes to William E. Borah, July 6, 1921, in William E. Borah Papers (Library of Congress, Washington, D.C.), Box 630.

[8]Dahl, loc. cit., p. 893. [Refers to a different page of the Dahl article from that of n. 6.]

[9]Cole, Self-Government in Industry, p. 126. [Even though this is the last-mentioned title by Cole, since the page is different loc. cit. will not do. Nor will op. cit. identify the work, since two works have been cited.]

[10]Hughes to Borah, loc. cit. [Refers to the same letter mentioned in n. 7.]

CONTENT FOOTNOTES AND CROSS-REFERENCES

48. *Content footnotes.*—These sometimes consist entirely of the writer's explanation or amplification of the discussion in the text. More often than not, however, the material there presented is supported by references to works or to other parts of the same paper (cross-references). Any one of several ways of placing the references is permissible. The same scheme need not be followed throughout the paper, and in any given note the position which seems most appropriate may be selected. But for references coming at the ends of sentences, either the scheme of enclosing or that of not enclosing in parentheses should be followed consistently. Whether the reference is given in its full form or in abbreviated form will depend upon whether the work has been cited previously. The style of the abbreviated form must be that used throughout the paper (see sec. 47, p. 44).

[1]Professor D. T. Suzuki brings this out with great clarity in his discussions of "stopping" and "no-mindedness"; see, e.g., his chapter on "Swordsmanship" (Zen Buddhism and Its Influence on Japanese Culture [Kyoto: Eastern Buddhist Society, 1938]).

[2]Ernst Cassirer takes important notice of this in Language and Myth (New York: Harper & Bros., 1946), pp. 59–62, and offers a searching analysis of man's regard for things on which his power of inspirited action may crucially depend.

[3]By 1935 it was estimated that company-union coverage was nearly 60 per cent of union membership, compared with 40 per cent in 1932 (Millis and Montgomery, op. cit., p. 841).

[4]But the important Babcock and Wilcox case, involving "free-speech" policy, was decided by a three-man panel. Supra, chap. xii, p. 424.

49. *Quotations in footnotes.*—Quoted matter in footnotes—both that run into the text and that set off from the text of the note—must be enclosed in double quotation marks.

50. *Cross-references.*—These are used to refer to other parts of the paper. Frequently they may be no more than, e.g., *"Supra,* p. 9" or its English equivalent, "Above, p. 9." But the Latin and English terms should not be used alternatively.

V

Tables

If tables are to serve satisfactorily the purpose for which they are made, they not only must be accurately compiled but must be so arranged that they can be easily read and interpreted. To these ends careful spacing, lining, arrangement of headings, period leaders, and, finally, the placing of the tables with respect to the text all contribute.

51. *Placement.*—Ideally, a table should follow immediately after it is first mentioned in the text. But this is not always possible if other matters equally as important as position are considered, as they must be. It is only sensible to expect that tables a page or less in length will be presented in one piece. If, then, the place at which the table is first mentioned is so far down the page that the table in its entirety cannot be accommodated, the typist may well be puzzled, especially since the general rule is to fill all pages whenever possible. The only answer to the puzzle is to omit the table at the point of its first mention, continue the text following it to the end of the page, and put the table at the top of the next page. As a matter of fact, if space permits, the text should continue at the top of the second page until the end of a paragraph is reached; but this of course must not be done unless there is ample space both to complete the paragraph and to type the entire table.

A table over a page in length should be begun immediately

after its first mention in the text, since it would have to be divided in any case.

If a table is wider than can be accommodated on one page in regular position and therefore must be placed either the long way of the paper or on facing pages (see Tables 6 and 7), it can be introduced immediately following its first mention only if that mention should come at the bottom of a page. Since this rarely happens, the typing of the text must continue to the foot of the page, and the table be placed on the next page (or pages). The completing of a paragraph on the same page as the table is in this case not permissible, since textual matter should not appear on the same pages with either broadside tables or facing tables.

52. *Arrangement of tables more than a page in width.*—Wide tables may be placed broadside (see Table 6). The table number and the caption should be at the binding side of the page. If too wide to be accommodated broadside, a table may be arranged on two facing pages (see Table 7). The parts of the table must be of the same dimensions on both pages, and special care in typing will be required to insure the appropriate figure in each column being exactly in line with the item in the stub (i.e., first column) to which it belongs

Tables too wide to be accommodated on the $8\frac{1}{2} \times 11$-inch page in either of the ways described may be typed on two or more pages, which then may be pasted together and reduced to page size by a suitable photographic process; or, less satisfactorily for the use of any paper that is to be bound and placed in a library, a large table may be folded (see sec. 70, p. 66).

53. *Continuation of tables more than a page in length.*—Long tables may be continued from page to page. The table number and the caption are typed at the beginning of the table; the table number only on succeeding pages, written, e.g., "TABLE 2—*Continued.*" Ordinarily, the box headings above the columns are repeated on every page, but in a continued *broadside* table the box headings are not repeated on the second page (and the fourth, sixth, and so on, if the table is very long) if the pages are placed facing each other.

54. *Table number and caption.*—Center the word "TABLE —," in capital letters on a line by itself, with the number in Arabic numerals. Center the caption, also in captial letters, on the second space below the table number. If the caption is longer than the table is wide, set it in two or more lines, arranging in inverted-pyramid form and single-spacing. Single-space before beginning the first rule above the box headings.

If most of the tables in the paper have captions two or more lines in length, space will be saved and the appearance of the tables will be improved by typing the captions in a style different from that just described. Type the table number (written "TABLE —" as above) flush with the left-hand edge of the table, add a period and dash, and begin the caption, typing the first line and all succeeding lines except the last the full width of the table, and centering the last line. Capitalize only the first word and proper nouns and proper adjectives:

```
        TABLE 1.--The effect of graded concentrations of
        carcinogens on the growth of Lactobacillus 46 in
                    a semisynthetic medium
```

One style of caption must be used consistently throughout the paper.

Occasionally, a writer may think that a certain table requires no caption. If none is given, the reason for the omission should be a defensible one.

55. *Box headings.*—Center the first "box heading" above the stub. If a description or classification of the line headings in the stub would be difficult to express briefly, substitute the word "Item." The remaining box headings may consist of a single level, each standing above the column to which it applies, or, if required, of two or more levels above (spanner headings), each spanner heading standing above a group of subsumed headings (see Tables 3–5, 7). Center all the headings above the columns or the group of subsumed headings to which they apply, leaving the same amount of blank space (at least one) above and below, and also at either end of the longest line, of the individual headings.

Box headings may be typed broadside if necessary to conserve space. They should be set so as to read up from the bottom of the page (see Table 6). It will be seen that if a table is typed the long way of the paper, and the box headings are then typed vertically, the headings will be upside down when the page is in regular position. This is as it must be.

Single-space all the box headings.

Numbering of the headings will prove a convenience if the textual discussion refers to individual columns. The numbers should be placed in parentheses as the first line below the box headings. The heading above the stub should be numbered "(1)" and the subsequent headings in numerical sequence (see Table 3).

Follow a consistent scheme of capitalization of box headings in all the tables. This may be either capitalization of the first word and proper nouns and proper adjectives; or capitalization of the first and last words and all nouns, pronouns, adjectives, adverbs, and verbs.

56. *Cut-in headings.*—Sometimes the use of cut-in headings, as shown in Table 5 ("Males, Females"), will permit the combining of data in one table that without them would require two or more tables. Cut-in headings should be centered and capitalized to accord with the scheme used for the box headings.

57. *Stub.*—In general, capitalize only the first word and proper nouns and proper adjectives. If a runover is necessary in a line heading, indent to the third space. Items under a general heading should be similarly indented:

```
Expenses
   Rent  . . . . .
   Heat  . . . . .
   Electricity . .
```

The words "Total," "Mean," and "Average" in the stub should also be indented. If the open space between the stub and the first column is such that the eye does not travel easily from the line heading to the related figure or word in the column, period leaders should be used as guides (see Table 7).

58. *Omissions in columns.*—In a long column of figures, zero preceding a decimal may be omitted from all entries except the first and the last. Degree and dollar signs must be repeated at the top of each column and after every break of the column, such as rules above totals and cut-in headings. A blank space in a column should carry period leaders (see Table 7).

59. *Aligning in columns.*—Align all columns of figures by the decimal points. In columns containing dissimilar items, center the dissimilar items and align the decimal points of figures even though figures may be interspersed with other items (see Table 4). Align plus, minus, and plus-minus signs (see Table 5).

60. *Abbreviations and symbols.*—Although for the most part prohibited in text, abbreviations and symbols are legitimate space-saving devices in box headings and in the main body of tables, but not in the captions. Standard abbreviations should be used

if they exist, but the writer may devise abbreviations when they do not. Possibly ambiguous abbreviations should be explained in a note or a "key." Symbols that cannot be made with the typewriter should be inserted by hand, using permanent black ink (India preferred). A plus sign made with the hyphen and diagonal slash ($\neq$) is *not* an acceptable substitute. The hyphen made with the typewriter, and the vertical bar inserted in ink, is satisfactory.

61. *Footnotes to tables.*—Put all footnotes to tables immediately below the tables, not at the foot of the page with footnotes to the text. Begin the first note on the second space below the bottom rule, indenting the first line of each note, single-spacing within the note, and double-spacing between the individual notes. Because footnote indexes in tables usually follow numerals, small letters ("a," "b," etc.) rather than Arabic numerals should be used. If none of the tables in the paper has more than one footnote, an asterisk may be used instead of "a," but the use of doubled and tripled asterisks, or of an asterisk part of the time and letters part of the time, should be avoided.

62. *Ruling.*—Two-column tables should be left completely unruled (see Table 1). In general, all tables of more than two columns should be ruled, as shown in the samples following Table 1. Put a double rule at the top and a vertical double rule between sections of a table that is doubled (see Table 2). Normally, no other double rules should be used. As has been said (see sec. 55, p. 53), a blank space should be left on all sides of box headings. It is never permissible to begin a heading on the line immediately below a rule, or to rule immediately under a heading (thus giving the effect of underlining of the words). The rule above the figures for totals, means, and averages should not be extended through the stub (see Table 3). In a table continued from page to page, the bottom rule should be omitted on all pages except the last.

Normally, horizontal rules are made with the typewriter; vertical rules, by hand (using permanent black ink, preferably India). If the carriage of the typewriter takes the paper the long way, all the rules may be made with the typewriter. Using the typewriter for the vertical rules will require particular care if the columns are only one or two spaces apart.

63. *Spacing.*—Mention of the proper spacing for captions, box headings, and footnotes has been made in the individual sections given to those topics. Other rules to be observed are the following: Three spaces should be left above and three spaces below (i.e., typing should begin on the third space below) tables inserted into text. Typing of the main body of the tables may be either single space or double space or space and one-half, and it need not be the same for all.

TABLE 1

DISTRIBUTION
OF INTERVIEW SCORES

Range and Scores	Frequency
79-75	1
74-70	2
69-65	6
64-60	5
59-55	16
54-50	10
49-45	3
44-40	5
39-35	2

TABLE 2

CASES FILED, TERMINATED, AND PENDING IN THE COURT OF APPEALS
FOR THE THIRD CIRCUIT, FISCAL YEARS 1940-1949, INCLUSIVE

Fiscal Year	Com-menced	Termi-nated	Pend-ing	Fiscal Year	Com-menced	Termi-nated	Pend-ing
1940	322	360	170	1945	299	268	226
1941	285	350	102	1946	197	274	149
1942	292	222	172	1947	266	216	199
1943	353	302	223	1948	287	250	236
1944	276	304	195	1949 (1st half)	128	113	251

TABLE 3

ADULT OFFSPRING OF 244 ARKANSAS FARM FAMILIES
BY EDUCATION AND PLACE OF RESIDENCE

Schooling (Years)	Living on Farms		Living in Towns	
	Individuals		Individuals	
	Number (2)	Percentage (3)	Number (4)	Percentage (5)
(1)				
8 or less	350	71[a]	211	60[a]
Above 8	142	29	139	40
10 and over	105	21	116	33
12 and over	62	13	72	21
14 and over	9	2	33	9
16 and over	3	1	15	4
Total	492	. .	. .	. .

[a]All differences over 3 times Standard Error.

TABLE 4

CHLOROPHYLL IN LEAF BLADES OF TOMATO

	April 26 Initial Plants	May 5 Minus-Nitrogen			May 5 Plus-Nitrate		
		50° F.	70° F.	95° F.	55° F.	70° F.	95° F.
As percentage of green matter	0.048	0.033	0.054	0.048	0.039	0.099	0.078
Relative values[a]	48	33	55	48	39	100	79

[a]Calculated using the plus-nitrate 70° F. plants, on May 5, as 100.

TABLE 5

EFFECT OF A SINGLE 24-HOUR EXPOSURE TO 33 DEGREES C. DURING
DIFFERENT PERIODS OF PUPAL DEVELOPMENT,
REMAINDER OF TIME AT 25 DEGREES C.

Period at 33 Degrees	No. Flies Emerged	Time in Days			Percentage of Development					
		Low Temp.	High Temp.	Total	Per Day		Low Temp.	High Temp.	Total	Total -100
					Low Temp.	High Temp.				
Males										
First day	61	3.31	1.00	4.31±0.009	23.47	27.54	77.68	27.54	105.22	+5.22
Second day	64	3.27	1.00	4.27±0.009	23.47	27.54	76.74	27.54	104.28	+4.28
Third day	62	3.14	1.00	4.14±0.020	23.47	27.54	73.69	27.54	101.23	+1.23
Fourth day	66	3.00	0.92	3.92±0.005	23.47	27.54	70.41	25.33	95.74	-4.26
Females										
First day	39	3.08	1.00	4.08±0.009	24.87	28.57	76.59	28.57	105.16	+5.16
Second day	53	2.94	1.00	3.94±0.006	24.87	28.57	73.11	28.57	101.68	+1.68
Third day	58	2.82	1.00	3.82±0.011	24.87	28.57	70.13	28.57	98.70	-1.30
Fourth day	51	3.00	0.86	3.66±0.007	24.87	28.57	74.64	24.57	99.21	-0.79

TABLE 6

VALUE ADDED BY MANUFACTURE PER PRODUCTION WORKER (IN DOLLARS), SOUTH BEND STANDARD METROPOLITAN AREA AND SEVEN SELECTED STANDARD METROPOLITAN AREAS, 1947[a]

Census Groups and Code Number	South Bend	South Bend Rank among Selected Standard Metropolitan Areas	Chicago	Indianapolis	St. Louis	Detroit	Toledo	Grand Rapids	Milwaukee
20. Food & kindred products	9,183	5	9,340	8,585	8,777	8,296	7,600	7,709	11,932
23. Apparel & related products	3,797	11	5,397	5,017	4,588	5,170	4,495	5,081	4,732
24. Lumber & products, except furniture	5,629	2	5,503	3,700	4,464	7,569	5,124	5,168	5,262
26. Paper & allied products	7,111	6	6,605	7,286	5,781	6,491	6,629	7,858	7,804
27. Printing & publishing industries	9,767	4	9,125	10,040	8,660	11,528	10,350	8,990	7,888
32. Stone, clay & glass products	4,033	11	6,558	6,058	5,663	6,563	10,284	6,049	6,383
33. Primary metal industries	6,397	4	6,689	4,321	5,599	5,600	6,668	5,263	6,453
34. Fabricated metal products	5,351	10	6,534	5,037	5,687	6,569	5,759	5,884	6,928
35. Machinery, except electrical	6,048	10	6,656	5,502	5,756	6,847	7,298	7,022	6,368
36. Electrical machinery	6,613	6	6,682	6,614	6,054	6,862	5,823	.[b]	6,243
39. Miscellaneous manufactures	4,755	7	6,042	5,521	4,760	5,825	4,608	5,239	4,642

[a]Calculated from: U.S. Department of Commerce, Bureau of the Census, Census of Manufactures: 1947 (Washington: U.S. Government Printing Office), Vol. III, Statistics by States, pp. 205-9, 306-8, 343-50, 479-81, 483, 648-49.

[b]Complete figures are not provided by the Census.

TABLE 7

CASE LOAD PER JUDGESHIP FOR THE NORTHERN DISTRICT OF FLORIDA
FOR THE FISCAL YEARS 1940-1948, INCLUSIVE
(CASES FILED PER JUDGE)

Fiscal Year	Number of Judges, Florida (Northern)	Total Civil Cases per Judge		Criminal Cases per Judge	
		Florida (Northern)	84 Districts	Florida (Northern)	84 Districts
1940	1	95	153	191	178
1941	1	104	164	247	165
1942	1	103	168	147	174
1943	1	79	158	105	190
1944	1	70	169	161	211
1945	1	98	295	239	209
1946	1	131	321	125	171
1947	1	106	271	110	173
1948	1	85	205	206	167

Notes:

During the entire period covered by the table there were 3 judges assigned to the southern district of Florida and 1 to the northern district. In
all these years except the fiscal year 1948, there was 1 "roving judge" for
both districts, but as almost all his time was spent in the southern district
the case load for 1940-48 has been figured on the basis of 1 judge in the
northern district.

Because case-load figures are given to the nearest whole number, it is
not always possible to derive exact totals by adding component parts.

TABLE 7--Continued

United States Civil Cases per Judge (United States a Party)						Private Civil Cases per Judge, Total	
Total		OPA		Other United States		Florida (Northern)	84 Districts
Florida (Northern)	84 Districts	Florida (Northern)	84 Districts	Florida (Northern)	84 Districts		
61	72	. .	. .	61	72	34	81
59	83	. .	. .	59	83	45	82
70	91	. .	. .	70	91	33	77
49	100	. .	12	49	88	30	58
47	113	7	37	40	76	23	56
70	238	6	160	64	78	28	57
103	251	71	174	32	77	28	70
80	162	30	84	50	78	26	109
63	87	6	20	57	67	22	117

VI

Illustrations

In addition to tables, illustrative materials may consist of graphs—
"pies," "curves," and map graphs—charts showing organization of
departments, plans, etc., diagrams of machines and instruments,
maps, photographs, commercial illustrations, and original illustrations.

It is not within the scope of this manual to give advice on the inclusion of illustrative materials, or on what type or types to use, or,
except in general terms, to give instructions on their presentation.
These matters are fully treated in a number of specialized books
and manuals.[1] Some general principles of preparation and presentation need to be summarized to bring the form of illustrative materials
into harmony with that of the text.

64. *Margins.*—A margin of at least one inch (more is permissible)
    should be allowed on all four sides of a page carrying illustrative
    material. Descriptive matter, legend or caption—everything but
    the page numbers—must fall within the margin.

65. *General form of presentation.*—Line graphs and bar charts
    may be either (1) drawn in India ink on cross-ruled paper of the
    same, or approximately the same, quality as the paper used

[1] Two may be mentioned: American Society of Mechanical Engineers, *Report of the Joint Committee on Standards for Graphic Presentation* (New York: A.S.M.E., 1918); Herbert Arkin and Raymond L. Colton, *Graphs, How To Make and Use Them* (rev. ed.; New York: Harper & Bros., 1940).

for the text; (2) drawn first on cross-ruled paper, traced on the plain bond paper, and the lines inked in; or (3) drawn first and then reproduced by a suitable photographic process. If several copies must be made, this last is the least time-consuming method, and it has the additional advantage of permitting the original drawing to be made larger than the normal page size, as is often desirable if there is fine detail to be shown.

Diagrams and some types of original illustrations may be similarly treated, except of course that plain bond paper or drawing paper slightly heavier than the bond, instead of cross-ruled paper, would be used.

Photographs either should be made in the $8\frac{1}{2} \times 11$-inch size, so as to avoid mounting, or be made smaller—possibly to allow for the placing of two or more on a page—and mounted upon the bond paper.

Commercial illustrations usually require mounting. If several copies of these are needed, and are not available, the originals may be reproduced photographically. If they are in color, however, photographs may not be satisfactory. The inclusion of illustrations in color may require considerable forethought. As a matter of fact, color cannot be used in a thesis or dissertation for a university or college which requires a planographic or microphotographic reproduction of its theses and dissertations. The photographs and photographic reproductions for use in such theses or dissertations should preferably be on glossy paper.

Many kinds of maps are available ready made, and some may serve satisfactorily with no additions except page and figure number and, possibly, a caption. Some may be used as base maps, with crosshatching, outlining of specific areas, "spotting," figures or letters superimposed to produce illustrations adequate for the writer's particular purposes. A thin, gummed paper with printed crosshatching on the reverse side, called Zip-a-tone, is available in many different styles of both the cross and the dot variety. For maps which are to be reproduced photographically before insertion in the paper, Zip-a-tone is a satisfactory substitute for handwork, but, since it has a tendency to come loose after a time, it should not be used in a piece of work designed to be kept for any considerable period.

Maps will of course many times need to be executed entirely by hand. In the fields of geography and geology, where knowledge of maps and mapmaking is so important an objective in the student's training, handmade maps in theses and dissertations, at least, are likely to be a requirement.

66. *Handwork.*—Legends, keys, captions, and any necessary lines, letters, or symbols not present in the illustration proper may be made either with the typewriter or by hand, using India ink. Lettering, if hand-done, should be clearly and evenly executed and spaced. As has been said, the use of color is not always feasible, and, when it is not, various styles of lines must be used in graphs employing two or more curves; and crosshatching, shading with dots and smaller circles, or similar devices should be used in bar charts. Zip-a-tone may replace handwork if the material is to be photographically reproduced.

67. *Legends and captions.*—If a paper contains several types of illustrations such as graphs, charts, maps, diagrams, it is desirable to label them all figures and number consecutively in Arabic numerals. If there is a disproportionately large number of one type, this should be given its own label and numbered in Arabic numerals in a separate series: "Map 1," "Chart 10," "Graph 15." The number and legend may be centered below the illustration in one of the following styles. The first is suitable for a short figure legend; the second, for a long one.

Fig. 1.--Block diagram of Fern Lake

Fig. 4.--Diagram of gross abnormalities observed in guinea pigs approximately 130 days after infection by one of 6 different strains of Br. abortus.

If the margin below the illustration is not deep enough to carry the figure legend and still allow the one inch of free space, the figure number may be typed at the top center or at the right in the open space surrounding the illustration proper. Sometimes illustrations—maps in particular—carry printed or hand-lettered captions at the top or side, in which case the figure number alone should be centered beneath the illustration.

A key or scale of miles, if included, ordinarily should be typed in a convenient open space surrounding the illustration rather than below it.

Normally full-page illustrations—especially photographic representations in light and shadow—should be labeled plates and numbered in capital Roman numerals (e.g., "PLATE VI") centered above the illustration.

If a plate is composed of more than one illustration, these may be individually labeled, either with a figure number alone or with both figure number and legend. If there are many figures on the page and each requires a legend, the illustrations may be numbered, and the figure legends either grouped at the foot of the page or placed on the facing page. A page containing several illustrations, each with its figure legend, need not be labeled a plate; but, for easy reference to the group as a whole, the plate number is a convenience.

A plate may carry a title or not, as may be desired. If it does, the title may be centered (in capital letters throughout) either above or below the illustration; the plate number remains at the top. If there is not space for the title and/or the plate number on the page with the illustration, these may be centered on the facing page. Since typing on photographic paper is not satisfactory, the labeling of a full-page illustration on sensitized paper will have to be done on the facing page.

68. *Placement.*—In general, illustrations should follow as closely as possible the first references to them in text. As with tables (see sec. 51, p. 50), these preferred positions are not always possible, and in some papers there may be sound reasons for grouping all the illustrations, if they are of one type, at the end. If there is a frontispiece, it should face the title page.

Either singly or in groups, illustrations may be placed the long way of the paper if this arrangement is better suited to their proportions. The appropriate label (plate number and title, or figure legend) should be typed broadside, so as to appear directly above or below the illustration, as may be suitable for its type. The top of the illustration should be at the binding side, and the page number should occupy its normal position.

69. *Mounting.*—Illustrations smaller than the normal page must be mounted on the bond typing paper. Stationers' rubber cement or dry mounting tissue should be the adhesive used. In using the cement, it is necessary to coat each surface (back of picture and area on the paper the picture will occupy) *twice.* It is not sufficient to put the cement only along the edges or at the corners, and care must be taken that there are no uncoated spots. Unlike most adhesives, any cement running beyond the edges of the picture can be rubbed off and will leave no trace unless it touches typing, which it will practically obliterate. Mounting done on text pages will require special care. Instructions for the use of dry mounting tissue accompany the material. Materials mounted with rubber cement should be thoroughly dried before being placed between typed pages. The pages of mounted material, each page protected by a piece of plain paper, should be placed under a weight for several hours, then exposed separately to the air for an hour or more.

70. *Folding.*—Illustrations larger than the normal page size may usually be reduced photographically. If reduction is not feasible, as it may not be in the case of large maps, for example, the material may be folded, provided that the institution for which the paper is prepared does not prohibit folding.

To fold, work first from right to left, making the first crease no more than 7½ inches from the left side of the sheet. If a second fold is necessary, carry the right-hand portion of the sheet back to the right, making the second crease no more than 6½ inches to the left of the first. Additional folds, if required, should be parallel with the first two. If the folding is done as directed, when the large folded sheet is in place, there will be no danger of the folds at the left being caught in the stitching or of those at the right being sheared off in the process of trimming. Folding in more than one direction should be avoided, but, if it is not possible to do so, the sheet should first be folded from bottom to top, making the first fold no more than 10 inches from the top of the sheet. When this first fold has been made, a strip 1 inch wide should be cut from the upper portion of the sheet (i.e., the portion that has been folded up), along the left edge, from the top down to the bottom fold. The removal of this strip is necessary to prevent the free portion of the sheet from being caught in the stitching. The folding from right to left should be as directed above.

71. *Numbering of pages.*—Pages of illustrative materials should be numbered consecutively with the textual matter. It is not permissible to insert them after the text has been numbered by giving them supplementary numbers (e.g., 45*a*). A folded sheet is numbered in the center at the top of the exposed fold.

VII

Scientific Papers

It is difficult to generalize about the format of scientific papers as distinct from other kinds of scholarly papers, not only because practice varies somewhat from field to field, but also because even within the same field variable factors determine style to some extent. In general, however, there are three major differences between format in non-scientific and in scientific papers: (1) organization, (2) handling of references, and (3) use of numerals, symbols, and abbreviations.

In such mechanical matters as spacing and pagination, and the presentation of tables and other illustrative materials, the scientific paper should conform in general to the style recommended in this manual under the several headings.

72. *Organization.*—The length of the paper determines quite largely whether it is typed continuously, that is, without beginning new pages for each major section, as is common in most short papers; whether each major section begins on a new page, without, however, formally designating each section as chapter or part; or whether each section, designated as chapter or part, begins on a new page, as is generally the practice in a long paper.

In the first two types, the major divisions may or may not be both numbered and titled, but properly they should be marked by either number or title. In all three types subheadings usually appear within the major divisions, but, in general, these should not begin new pages. (Suitable styles of subheadings and some suggestions on their logical order are discussed in sec. 10, pp. 6–7.)

In short papers it is not necessary to include a table of contents, a list of tables, or a list of illustrations, although individual preferences or the demands of a particular piece of writing may call for one or all of these tables.

73. *References.*—In papers in scientific fields, the general practice is to collect all the references at the end of the paper under some such heading as "List of References" or "Literature Cited." The term "Bibliography" appears less often, since for the most part it is not appropriate, the "List" usually being confined to those works mentioned in the paper. If the list actually is a bibliography, it should be so headed.

Under the "list scheme" (regardless of its heading), one of two styles of reference index in the text is most common:

a) An Arabic numeral placed between parentheses (sometimes between square brackets [ ]) on the line with the text, the number agreeing with the specific reference in the List of References. The references run in numerical order through the paper, but this order may be interrupted when necessary to cite again an earlier reference. The List of References is ordinarily arranged numerically. If an alphabetical arrangement is desired, the references must be numbered after the entries have been alphabetized. It follows that numerical order of the text indexes is not possible if the List is arranged alphabetically.

Although under this scheme of handling references, the style of entry in the list varies somewhat among fields, the following serve as patterns:

Article

1. ADAMS, J. Some further experiments on the relation of light to growth. Amer. Jour. Bot. 12:398-412. 1925.

Book

7. BRITTON, N. L., and BROWN, A. An Illustrated Flora of the Northern United States, Canada, and the British Possessions. Vol. 2. Charles Scribner's Sons, New York. 1913.

b) The year-date of the publication placed in parentheses on the line with text and usually following immediately the name of the author. If the author's name is not brought into the sentence, it must, of course, be placed within the parentheses, preceding the year-date. Under this scheme, the List of References is arranged alphabetically. If it contains two or more works by the same author, the works of such authors are listed chronologically. Two or more works by the same author published in the same year are identified as, e.g., "1950[a]," "1950[b]," etc. Unless there is a purpose to be served by numbering the entries, numbering is omitted.

Suggested styles of entries are the following:

Article

ALLEE, E. C. 1934. Recent studies in mass physiology. Biol. Rev., 9:1-48.

Book

DAVIES, O. L. 1947. Statistical methods in research and production, pp. 51-70. London: Oliver & Boyd.

Under either scheme, if reference to specific parts of a work—chapters, pages, tables, illustrations—is desired, the notation follows the reference number or the reference date within the parentheses. For example:

Brown shows (7, Table 4) that . . .

Ulrich (1927, p. 29 and Fig. 2) divided the Simpson . . .

In the foregoing examples of entries in a List of References, the title of the article is included in the entry. In some fields it is usual to omit the title of the article. Names of journals are commonly given in abbreviated form. The decision whether titles of articles are to be used should be made before the List of References is compiled, and a consistent scheme should be followed. Also, the standard abbreviations used for the journals should be followed throughout the list. Volume numbers usually appear in Arabic numerals, although some journals use Roman numerals for volume numbers of books. If the paper is to be submitted to a specific journal for publication, it is well to follow exactly the style of reference used by that journal.

Although the practice of collecting the references in a list at the end of the paper appears to be growing in use, it is by no means uniform even within a given field, and the citing of references in footnotes is not uncommon. They follow the same general pattern of an entry in a List of References except that the author's name usually is given in regular order—Mark E. Jones, not Jones, Mark E. The reference index is usually a superscript numeral, agreeing with the numeral identifying the note. These numerals may begin with "1" on each page, or they may run consecutively through the entire paper.

The styles of references illustrated by the following examples are for entries in a List of References in some cases and for footnotes in others. They are the styles used by leading publications in the several fields.

a) *Anthropology*—textual and bibliographical references.

In this field there is some variation in practice. The scheme of the *American Anthropologist* is cited here. References to literature are given in the text of the paper. The author's surname (unless it is brought into the text), year-date of the publication, and page number are enclosed in parentheses: "(Herskovits 1952: 12–14)." A bibliography at the end of the paper supplies complete information in the following forms:

(1) Journal reference:

BIDNEY, D.
1950   The Concept of Myth and the Problem of
        Psychocultural Evolution. American
        Anthropologist 52:16-26.

(2) Book reference:

KROEBER, ALFRED L.
1952   The Nature of Culture. Chicago, Univer-
                      sity of Chicago Press.

b) *Botany*—list of references: *see* examples under *a*), page 69.

c) *Chemistry*—footnote references

   (1) Journal reference:

(8) S. R. Palit, J. Org. Chem., 12, 752 (1947).

   (2) Book reference:

(4) C. H. Goulden, "Methods of Statistical Analysis," 2d ed.,
     John Wiley and Sons, Inc., New York, N.Y., 1952, p. 42.

d) *Geology*—entries in list of references

   (1) Journal reference:

COOKE, C. W. (1930) Pleistocene seashores: Washington Acad.
Sci. Jour., vol. 20, p. 389-395.

   (2) Book reference:

KRUMBEIN, W. C., and PETTIJOHN, F. G. (1938) Manual of sedimen-
tary petrography, New York, D. Appleton-Century Co., Inc.

e) *Mathematics*—list of references

   (1) Journal reference:

12. O. Ore, <u>Contributions to the theory of finite fields</u>, Trans.
     Amer. Math. Soc. vol. 36 (1934) pp. 243-74.

   (2) Book reference:

7. E. Landau, <u>Vorlesungen über Zahlentheorie</u> vol. II, Leipzig,
    1927.

f) *Physics*—footnote references

   (1) Journal reference:

[9]J. H. Van Vleck, J. Chem. Phys. 5, 320 (1937).

   (2) Book reference:

[7]F. Seitz, <u>Modern Theory of Solids</u> (McGraw-Hill Book Co., Inc.,
New York, 1940), p. 414.

g) Psychology—list of references

(1) Journal reference:

1. Archer, P. W. The tactile perception of roughness. <u>Amer. J.</u>
<u>Psychol</u>., 1950, <u>63</u>, 365, 373.

(2) Book reference:

9. Jackson, J. Y. <u>The psychology of industrial unrest</u>. New
York: McGraw-Hill, 1948.

h) Zoölogy—list of references: *see* examples, page 70 (Allee,
Davies).

74. *Content footnotes.*—Relevant material not of sufficient importance to be brought into the text of the paper may be put into
footnotes. When the scheme adopted is to put the references
to the literature into footnotes, content footnotes should be
numbered consecutively with the reference footnotes. When
the scheme is to put all the references to the literature into a
list at the end of the paper, the content footnotes should be
numbered separately, beginning with "1" and numbering them
consecutively through the entire paper. To distinguish them
clearly from the references to the literature, these content
footnotes should be indicated by superscript Arabic numerals.
It is bad form to put the content footnotes into the List of
References. In general, the use of asterisks to refer to text
footnotes is not advisable.

75. *Numerals, symbols, and abbreviations.*—The demand in scientific
papers for the use of numbers and units of measurement
expressed in numerical values makes it suitable for purposes
of clarity to use figures, symbols, and abbreviations to an extent
not considered good form in non-scientific writing. Aside from
a few rules here set down, the writer must settle on the scheme
he will use—preferably when working on his first draft—and
maintain the same usage throughout the paper.

a) Spell out a number at the beginning of a sentence, even if it is part of a connected group for which numerals are used after it. A better plan in such circumstances is to reconstruct the sentence so as not to begin with a number.

b) Spell out expressions of measurement when they are not preceded by numbers.

c) To avoid confusion, spell out one set of figures in an expression involving two or more series of figures:

> "In a test given six months later, ninety-seven children made no errors; eighty-two made 1-2 errors; sixty-four made 3-4 errors. . . ."

d) Do not use the symbol for *per cent* (%) when it is not preceded by a figure. *Percentage*, not *per cent* nor %, is the correct expression to use when no figure is given:

> "The September scores showed an improvement of 70.1% [or 70.1 per cent if the writer prefers to spell out]. Thus the percentage of achievers in the second test indicated. . . ."

In mathematical text the demands for the use of symbols and abbreviations are so complicated, and vary so much from one paper to another, that no suggestions can be given here. Students in this field should receive training in correct usage along with their education in the science. Editors of some of the mathematical periodicals have prepared manuals for authors which give useful suggestions.

VIII

The Appendix and the Bibliography

76. *The appendix* stands in somewhat the same relation to the paper as content footnotes in that it provides a place for material that is not absolutely necessary to the text. In it may be placed tables too detailed for text presentation; technical notes on method, and schedules and forms used in collecting materials; copies of documents not generally available to the reader; case studies too long to be put into text; and sometimes illustrative materials. If the materials thus relegated to an appendix are numerous in each of several categories, each category should form a separate appendix. Thus the appendixes would be numbered or lettered (I, II, etc., or A, B, etc.). Each may bear a title or not, as may be desired.

77. *The bibliography* lists the sources used in the preparation of the paper, not necessarily every work examined but those that were found relevant. In some cases the writer may prefer to include only a selected bibliography, omitting the less complete or less useful sources. Such sources as personal interviews, lectures, and radio talks, although not actually bibliographical materials, are by common usage included in a bibliography for the sake of convenience.

78. *Classification.*—The bibliography is usually classified according to the several types of publications and other sources used, and for some papers the variety of materials may suggest subheadings under the main classifications. Within each classification (and subsections if any) the entries should be arranged according to a definite order. Alphabetical order by author is the most common, although a chronological order is sometimes used. An author may be an individual or individuals, a committee, department, agency, state or country, etc.

The entry of a work for which there is no author begins with the title, and its position in the bibliography is determined by the initial word of the title exclusive of an article.

When two or more works by the same author appear in succession, a continuous line eight spaces in length, followed by a period, may be substituted for the author's name after its first appearance (see entries for Cole, p. 79).

79. *Arrangement and punctuation of individual entries.*—The arrangement of the items of a bibliographical entry is essentially the same as that of a footnote (see sec. 22 *a*, *b*, pp. 20–21) except that the surname comes first, followed by a comma and the given name or initials. The full name ends with a period, which will be the same period as that following an initial if the given name ends with an initial. From this point on, the entry for an article in a periodical is the same as that of a footnote. Entries for books and other publications show a period instead of a comma after the title, and the facts of publication are not enclosed in parentheses.

80. *Capitalization and underlining.*—Capitalization must agree with the scheme adopted for the citing of titles in footnotes and elsewhere in the paper (see sec. 28, p. 29).

In the bibliography underlining of the titles of whole publications—books, periodicals, and all other works whose titles are underlined in footnotes—is optional. The quoting of titles of articles and of component parts of whole publications is necessary. Foreign words and phrases must be underlined; except that titles entirely in a foreign language are not underlined if the option is taken of not underlining the titles of whole publications. Nor is a "quoted" titled entirely in a foreign language underlined.

81. *Notation of total number of pages.*—Some institutions and some departments may require that entries of books and pamphlets include the total number of pages in each work. If there is such a notation, it should indicate the preliminary pages and the pages of text separately, e.g., "Pp. xiv+450." For periodical articles, the inclusive pages should be shown.

82. *Indentation.*—For ease of reference it is desirable that the author's name should stand out, and prominence is given by placing the name flush with the margin and indenting succeeding lines of each entry a definite number of spaces, observing the same indentation for all entries. In general, indentation of from four to eight spaces is satisfactory.

If desired, the authors' names can be given further prominence by typing in capitals throughout.

83. *Spacing.*—This may be either double, single, or one and one-half. If single, there should be a double space between entries.

84. *Annotation.*—If the bibliographical entries are annotated, the annotation should be typed in single spacing and should begin on the line following the entry proper:

Thompson, Oscar (ed.). <u>International Cyclopedia of Music and Mu-sicians</u>. New York: Dodd, Mead & Co., 1938.
      An admirable work which brings Grove up to date and deals adequately with contemporary music and American composers.

85. *Examples of bibliographical entries.*—The following examples are chosen for the purpose of showing a variety of styles of entry, rather than a sample bibliography. For convenience the entries are placed under appropriate headings, which suggest one, but by no means the only kind of classification. The kinds of source materials used and, to some extent, the number of each kind should determine the classification or absence of it.

Public Documents

Commonwealth of Massachusetts. Report of the Governor's Labor-Management Committee. House of Representatives No. 1875. March 18, 1947.

Great Britain. Hansard's Parliamentary Debates (3d series). Vols. CLVIII-CLXVI.

Great Britain. Parliamentary Debates (5th series). (Commons.) Vol. LXXVI (1915).

Great Britain. Parliamentary Papers. Vol. XIX (Accounts and Papers, Vol. VII). Cmd. .3157. July, 1928.

Great Britain. Public Record Office. Calendar of State Papers, Colonial Series, America and the West Indies, 1733.

Great Britain. Public Record Office. Calendar of State Papers Relating to Scotland and Mary, Queen of Scots, 1547-1603. Vol. VII (1585-86).

Great Britain. Trade Disputes and Trade Unions Act, 1946. Statutes at Large. 9 and 10 George VI (1946).

Great Britain. Statutes at Large. 26-30 George II (1753-56). Vol. XXI.

U.S. Bureau of the Census. Seventeenth Census of the United States: 1940. Population, Vol. II.

U.S. Congress, Joint Committee on Labor-Management Relations. Hearings on Operation of Labor-Management Relations Act of 1947. 80th Cong., 2d Sess., 1948.

U.S. Congressional Record. Vol. LXXXV.

U.S. House of Representatives. Conference Report, Labor-Management Relations Act, 1947. Report No. 510. 80th Cong., 1st Sess.. June 3, 1947.

U.S. President, 1945-53 (Truman). The National Emergency: Address and Proclamation, Washington, D.C., Dec. 15 and 16, 1950. Department of State Publication No. 4052.

U.S. Senate, Committee on Labor. Minority Report, Proposed Amendments to the National Labor Relations Act. Report No. 1928, Part 3, 76th Cong., 3d Sess., 1940.

U.S. Statutes at Large. Vol. XXIV.

Books

Aaron, Daniel. Men of Good Hope: A Story of American Progressives. New York: Oxford University Press, 1951.
[Here the subtitle as well as the main title is underlined. The writer may choose to omit underlining of subtitles throughout the paper.]

Adams, Herbert Baxter. Bluntschli's Life-Work. Baltimore: Privately printed, 1884.

Adams, Joseph Quincy (ed.). Chief Pre-Shakespearean Dramas. Boston: Houghton Mifflin Co., 1924.

Anderson, J. N. D. (ed.) The World's Religions. London: Inter-Varsity Fellowship, 1950.

Aristotle. Constitution of Athens and Related Texts. Translated with an introduction and notes by Kurt von Fritz and Ernst Kapp. (Hafner Library of Classics, No. 13.) New York: Hafner Publishing Co., 1950.

Chamberlain, Joseph P., Dowling, Noel T., and Hayes, Paul R. The Judicial Function in Federal Administrative Agencies. New York: Commonwealth Fund, 1942.

Chamberlin, T. C., and Salisbury, R. D. Geology. Vol. I: Geologic Processes and Their Results. 2d ed. revised. New York: Henry Holt & Co., 1906.

Chesterton, G. K. Robert Browning. "English Men of Letters." New York and London: Macmillan Co., 1903.

Cole, G. D. H. Self-Government in Industry. 5th ed. revised. London: G. Bell & Co., Ltd., 1920.

_____. A Short History of the British Working Class Movement. 3 vols. New York: Macmillan Co., 1927.

Dutcher, G. M., et al. [Or Dutcher, G. M., and Others] Guide to Historical Literature. New York: Macmillan Co., 1931.

Falloux, Frédéric Alfred Pierre, Comte de. Mémoires d'un royaliste. Paris: Perrin et Cie, 1888.

Gregory, Charles O., and Katz, Harold A. Policy Development under the National Labor Relations Act. Chicago: Industrial Relations Center, University of Chicago, 1947. (Processed.)

Latane, J. H. America as a World Power, 1897-1907. Vol. XXV of The American Nation: A History. Edited by A. B. Hart. New York: Harper & Bros., 1909.

Modern Humanities Research Association. Annual Bibliography of English Language and Literature. Vol. IX, 1928. Edited for the Modern Humanities Research Association by E. Seaton and M. S. Serjeantson. Cambridge: Cambridge University Press, 1929.

Moore, John Bassett. History and Digest of the International Arbitration to Which the United States Has Been a Party. 6 vols. (53d Cong., 2d sess.; H.R. Misc. Doc. 212.) Washington, D.C.: Government Printing Office, 1888.

Phillimore, Baron Walter G. F. Schemes for Maintaining General Peace. ("[Great Britain] Foreign Office Handbooks . . . ," No. 160; "Peace Handbooks," Vol. XXV, No. 3.) London: H.M. Stationery Office, 1920.

Raymond, Jean-Paul [C. Ricketts]. Oscar Wilde: Recollections. London: Nonesuch Press, 1932.

Stephen, Sir Leslie. The English Utilitarians. Vol. I: Jeremy Bentham. Vol. II: James Mill. Vol. III: John Stuart Mill. (Reprints of Scarce Works on Political Economy, Nos. 9-11.) London: London School of Economics and Political Science, 1950. (First published in 1900: New York, G. P. Putnam's Sons; London, Duckworth & Co.)

The Unit Method of Teaching. Edited by W. R. Smithey. ("Secondary Education in Virginia," No. 17; "University of Virginia Record Extension Series," Vol. XVII, No. 7.) Charlottesville, Va.: University Extension Department, University of Virginia, 1933.

Whitaker, Virgil K. The Religious Basis of Spenser's Thought. ("Stanford University Publications: Language and Literature," Vol. VII, No. 3.) Stanford, Calif.: Stanford University Press, 1950.

Articles and Periodicals

Acton, Richard Maximilian Dalberg, 2d Baron. Letter to the Editor, The Times (London), Oct. 28, 1906.

[Blank, Henry V.] "Art for Its Own Sake," The New Art in America, XXI (December, 1940), 63-67.

Drucker, Peter F. "The Employee Society," American Journal of Sociology, LVIII (January, 1953), 358-63. (Paper read before the Forty-seventh Annual Meeting of the American Sociological Society, at Atlantic City, N.J., Sept. 3, 1952.)

Jen Min Jih Pao (People's Daily, Peking), 1951, 1952.

"Jobs and Occupations: A Popular Evaluation," National Opinion Research Center, Opinion News, IX, No. 4 (September 1, 1947), 12-28.

Jonckheere, Frans. "Le Cadre professionnel et administratif des médecins égyptiens," Chronique d'Égypte, No. 52 (Juillet, 1951), pp. 248-49.

Kubler, George. "The Quechua in the Colonial World," in Handbook of South American Indians ("Bureau of American Ethnology Bulletins," No. 143 [6 vols.; Washington, D.C., 1946]), II, 331-410.

Labor Relations Reporter. Vols. I-XXIII. Washington: Bureau of National Affairs, 1935-48.

Miller, Bruce. "Conference at Baguio," Time and Tide (London), August 21, 1954.

New York Times. 1950-1954.

Roebuck, Carl. "The Economic Development of Ionia," Classical Philology, XLVIII (January, 1953), 9-16.

Viner, Jacob. "Cost Curves and Supply Curves," Zeitschrift für National-Okonomie, Band III (1932), 23ff.

Reports

American Medical Association. Medical Relations under Workmen's Compensation. A Report Prepared by the Bureau of Medical Economics. Chicago: American Medical Association, 1933.

Angell, James W. Financial Foreign Policy of the United States. A Report to the Second International Studies Conference on the State and Economic Life, London, May 29 to June 2, 1933. Prepared by the American Committee Appointed by the Council on Foreign Relations. New York, 1933.

Broadview College. Annual Reports of the President. 1900-1915.

Smithsonian Institution. Annual Report of the Board of Regents
for the Year Ending June 30, 1931. Washington: U.S.
Government Printing Office, 1933.

Trades Union Congress. Report of Eighty-first Annual Congress
(Bridlington, 1949). London: By the Trades Union Congress, 1949.

Unpublished Material

American Institute of Planners, Chicago Chapter. "Regional
Shopping Centers Planning Symposium." Chicago, 1942.
(Mimeographed.)

Carpenter, Irene Maude. "Construction of a Self-administering
Spelling Test." Unpublished Master's dissertation, Department of Education, University of Chicago, 1934.

David, Flavius Louis. "The Selection and Organization of Personnel for Curriculum Revision." Bulletin of Curriculum
Laboratory, No. 30. Cleveland, Ohio: School of Education, Western Reserve University, 1932. (Mimeographed.)

Miles, Ethel. "Girls' Reading Interests." Paper read before the
meeting of the Scarsdale Library Club, Scarsdale, N.Y.,
March 26, 1937.

Morristown (Kansas) Orphans' Home. Minutes of Meetings of Board
of Managers. 1925-1935. (Typewritten.)

Tatum, Edward Howland, Jr. "The United States and Europe, 1815-
1823: A Study in the Background of the Monroe Doctrine."
Unpublished Ph.D. dissertation, University of California,
1934.

Other Sources

Broadview College. Personal interviews with the President and
heads of Departments. October, 1942; May, 1943.

Farmers' State Bank, Barrett, Nebraska. Personal interviews with
selected list of depositors. August, 1930.

_____. Personal interview with Henry Y. Cage, President,
Farmers' State Bank, Barrett, Nebraska. July 10, 1930.

Appendix I

Typing the Paper

86. *The writer's responsibility for editing.*—Before final typing the writer should edit the paper. He alone is responsible for the correct presentation of the content and the reference and illustrative materials. The editing will save his time if he expects to do the typing himself, and it will save unnecessary errors, which would require correction in the final copy, involving both time and expense. Beyond the production of an accurate transcription of the copy, the typist should be held responsible only for mechanical details having to do with neatness, spacing, and the general appearance of the final copy.

87. *Typewriter.*—Either pica or elite type, or one of the type faces available on some of the newer models, is satisfactory for most typing jobs, although some institutions specify pica type for theses and dissertations. A typist who expects to do any considerable amount of typing of theses, dissertations, or other formal papers—particularly those designed for submission to publishers —would do well to provide herself with a specially equipped typewriter, preferably with pica type. The special vertical spacing obtainable with the five-line ratchet is recommended for the typing of copy that is to be reproduced by planographing (also called lithoprinting), and it may be used for any other copy, subject to the approval of the person for whom the copy is to be prepared. The same ratchet permits single and double spacing, and the accurate half-space turn of the roller is a great convenience in the typing of superscripts and subscripts. Keys with the grave accent mark (`), the acute accent mark (´), the plus symbol (+), the plus-and-minus symbol (±), and the square brackets ([ ]) are almost indispensable. Some of the symbols carried on the standard keyboard are used less frequently in the typing of formal papers than in commercial work and can be replaced with the more necessary symbols at a nominal charge.

The type should be kept clean with a special brush and cleaner made for the purpose, and the rollers (not the platen only, but small rollers as well) should be kept in good condition with a special cleaner. Periodically, a thorough check of the typewriter should be made by a responsibile serviceman to insure smooth rollers, uniformity of letter impression, alignment of letters, and proper adjustment of tension.

88. *Ribbon.*—Ribbons of superior quality are most satisfactory in the long run. Medium-inked black ribbons produce greater uniformity of impression than the light-inked or the heavy-inked. To secure superior uniformity of type color, it is desirable to have on hand before the typing is begun enough ribbons of the same kind to complete the job, and to rotate them at regular intervals of, say, every twenty-five pages. This is particularly desirable in typing copy for planographing.

89. *Paper.*—A good grade of bond paper should be used. Some institutions have specific requirements for theses and dissertations. If there are no such requirements, paper of 20-pound weight and at least 50 per cent rag content should be used. Some institutions permit a lighter weight for the carbon copies.

90. *Carbon paper.*—The carbon paper used should be of good quality: black, hard finish (non-greasy), light- or medium-weight (light-weight is preferable if several copies are to be made). Such carbon paper makes a gray rather than a black impression, but the letters are sharper, and the copies smudge less and remain in good condition longer than those made with paper of a soft or medium finish.

MECHANICS OF TYPING

91. *Margins.*—Leave a margin of at least one inch on each of the four sides of the sheet. Some institutions require more than this, particularly on the left, since binding reduces the margin. On the first page of every major division of the paper, leave two inches at the top above the heading.

92. *Indentation.*—Indent paragraphs six to eight spaces, unless specific regulations are made. Follow the same scheme of paragraph indentation consistently.

93. *Pagination.*—*Assign* a number to every page except the blank sheet following the title page. On the title page—and the half-title pages, if there are any—the numbers are not shown.

a) For the preliminaries, number with small Roman numerals (i, ii, iv, etc.) centered at the bottom of the page three-fourths of an inch above the edge. The numbering begins with "ii"; the title page counts as page i.

b) Number the remaining parts, including text, illustrations, appendix, and bibliography with Arabic numerals, centered at the top of the page three-fourths of an inch below the edge, except that on every page with a major heading (e.g., the first page of a chapter, or of the bibliography), place the number at the foot of the page, centered three-fourths of an inch above the edge. Begin the numbering of the main body with "1" and run consecutively to the end of the paper.

An alternate scheme of pagination is that of numbering all pages in the upper right-hand corner—except of course title page and half-title pages.

94. *New pages* (*where begun*).—Begin every major division (i.e., preface, contents, list of tables, list of illustrations, introduction, each new chapter, appendix, bibliography) on a new page.

95. *Major headings.*—Begin every major division with a major heading. This may or may not begin with a chapter number. If it does, center the chapter number on a line by itself two inches below the top (e.g., "CHAPTER I"). If the "chapter" is not formally expressed, the number and the title are centered two inches below the top (e.g., "I. THE CANAL LAND BOOM"). If the chapter and number are on a line alone, center the title on the third line below, using capital letters throughout. If the title is more than five inches in length (i.e., if it would extend to the left of the paragraph indentation), set it in two or more double-spaced lines, in inverted-pyramid form. Use no terminal punctuation at the end of the chapter number or of the title. Begin typing the text (or the subheading, if any) on the third space below the last line of the title.

96. *Subheadings.*—Because of their bearing on the organization of the text, subheadings in general, their various forms, and the order in which they should be used are discussed in the chapter on the text (sec. 10, pp. 6-7). Type centered headings over five inches in length in two or more single-spaced lines, in inverted-pyramid form. Type side headings over a half-line in length in two or more single-spaced lines, beginning each line flush with the margin. Use no terminal punctuation at the end of a subheading except a paragraph heading.

97. *Spacing of text and footnotes.*—Type the text either double space or space and one-half, as the writer may choose. Type the footnotes single space (see below, sec. 101, p. 88).

98. *Spacing between subheadings.*—Leave a triple space above every subheading but the last, exclusive of a paragraph heading (i.e., begin typing on the third line). Leave a double space between the last subheading and the text.

99. *Guide sheet.*—The preparation and use of the guide sheet is discussed in the section on the typing of footnotes (sec. 102, p. 89).

100. *Corrections and erasures.*—No interlineations, crossing-out of letters or words, strikeovers, or extensive erasures are permissible. Deletion or addition of more than one letter after the line has been completed should be made by retyping. By skilful use of the back-spacer, the letters of a word can be crowded so that the space normally occupied by a word of given length can be made to accommodate a word having one more letter. This must be done by erasing the entire word and reducing evenly the space between the letters, not by crowding just two letters. Extensive correction of a page once passed calls for great care in retyping so that the material may be equalized and the last line on the page properly spaced out to the end. Erasures should be reduced to a minimum and made with such skill on both the original and the copies that they will not be noticeable. Wherever possible they should be made before the set is removed from the typewriter. Typists should form the habit of looking over each page before removing it from the machine. Once withdrawn, each copy of the set should be corrected separately by direct type rather than all together by restacking and insertion of carbons. Care should be exercised to strike the keys heavily or lightly, as the case may require, so that the corrected portions may match in color as nearly as possible the remainder of the typed material upon the page.

An erasing shield and two ink erasers—one with a broad edge for covering larger areas and one with a narrow edge for the smaller ones—are indispensable. To prevent smudging of the face copy, the fingers should rest on the erasing shield. To prevent smudging of the carbon copies, a piece of paper should be placed between each sheet of carbon and the page beneath.

Corrections on copy prepared for planographing must not be made by erasing. If a mistake is made, the word or words should be retyped on a separate piece of paper and placed over the part to be corrected, attaching with rubber cement. Great care must be taken to place the "patch" accurately and neatly and to leave no dark lines or specks which would show in the printed copy. Typing the corrected material on white gummed paper is an alternative to typing on plain paper and pasting.

TYPING THE FOOTNOTES

101. *Spacing, indentation, footnote numeral.*—Separate text and footnotes with an unbroken line extending from margin to margin beneath the text and one space below it. The first line of footnote material is on the second line below this (the third line under the text). Indent the first line of each footnote the same number of spaces as the paragraph indentation in the text. Type the footnotes single space, but double-space between individual notes.

Place the footnote numeral slightly above the line (never a full space above). There should be no punctuation after the numeral and no extra space between it and the first of the note:

[1]G. D. H. Cole, Self-government in Industry, p. 16.

102. *How to gauge spacing of text and footnotes.*—To place the footnotes correctly on the page and maintain the proper margin at the foot of the page, a *guide sheet* should be used. This may be made of firm, light-weight wrapping paper. Cut it the same length as the typing paper and one-half inch wider. Measure off top and bottom margins to correspond with those used on the typed page, insert the paper into the typewriter, and, beginning with "1" on the line with that occupied by the first line of text on the typed page, number down the extreme right-hand edge of the guide sheet to the line opposite that of the last line of typed matter. It is helpful also to indicate in the top and bottom margins of the guide sheet the point opposite which the page number should appear (see sec. 93, p. 85).

Before rolling the paper and guide sheet into the typewriter, place the guide sheet back of the bottom sheet of typing paper; align the top and left-hand edges of paper, carbon paper, and guide sheet so that the numbered edge of the guide sheet extends beyond the typing paper; and roll the stacked paper into the typewriter. It may be necessary to adjust the top edges after the paper is placed in the machine.

When the first footnote number appears in the text, stop and count the number of lines in the corresponding footnote, add two to allow for the line of separation, and deduct this total from the total number of type lines as shown on the guide sheet. The difference between the two figures will give the number of the line at the end of which to stop typing text in order to allow proper space for the footnote. As each succeeding footnote number appears in the text, add the number of lines in the corresponding footnote, allowing one extra for the space between notes, and again determine the number of text lines to be typed.

All will go according to plan, and the bottom margin will be the proper depth unless a footnote number occurs in the last line of text after all available footnote space has been allotted.

Make it a habit to look ahead so as to discover such a difficulty, and avoid the necessity of retyping the page by omitting the last line, even though this will result in a bottom margin deeper than usual.

A similar difficulty arises when a footnote number shows the corresponding footnote to be longer than can be accommodated in the space remaining on the page. This calls for a division of the footnote.

103. *Continuation of a long footnote to the following page.*—Begin the note on the page where reference to it appears in the text and type as much as the page will allow, taking care to break the note within a sentence. Carry the remainder into the footnote area of the next page, where it precedes the footnotes for that page. To indicate the continuation of a footnote by such a statement as "Continued on the next page" is bad form.

104. *Arrangement of short footnotes.*—To avoid the unattractive appearance and the waste of space which result from the placement of many short footnotes, each on a line by itself and separated from its fellows by extra space above and below, it is advisable to let such short notes follow each other on the same line. There must, however, be at least three spaces between notes, and *all the notes on one line must be complete.* It is not permissible to carry over to the next line a part of the last note. Similarly, it is not permissible to utilize the blank space following a note of more than one line in length to insert a short note:

Wrong:
    [1]John Dove, <u>Confutation of Atheism</u>, p. 125.   [2]Ibid., pp. 128-29.

Wrong:
    [1]G. D. H. Cole, <u>Self-government in Industry</u> (5th ed. rev.; London: G. Bell & Co., 1920), p. 2.   [2]<u>Ibid</u>., p. 9.

Appendix II

Some Rules of Punctuation

105. This brief section on punctuation, covering only those rules most frequently violated, is provided for the convenience of students desiring to review this subject.

a) A period should be placed at the end of every complete declarative or imperative sentence, although two individual statements closely joined in thought may be linked together by a semicolon. The substitution of a comma for the period or the semicolon in such sentences as the following constitutes the "comma fault."

Wrong: The hour was late, we were obliged to go by automobile.
Right: The hour was late. We were obliged to go by automobile.

Wrong: Let us grant the evils of vicarious living, let us also grant its necessity.
Right: Let us grant the evils of vicarious living; let us also grant its necessity.

Wrong: At the end of two weeks thirty questionnaires had not been returned, therefore, another thirty were sent out to persons not on the original list.
Right: At the end of two weeks thirty questionnaires had not been returned; therefore, another thirty were sent out to persons . . .

Wrong: They wanted to check their revised opinions with me, with each other, in fact, they wanted to spend so much time that . . .

Right: They wanted to check their revised opinions with me, with each other; in fact, they wanted to spend so much time that . . .

b) Ordinarily, a comma should separate two independent clauses joined by "and," "but," "or," "nor" if a change of subject takes place.

Right: This was an ancient custom among the Greeks, and the Romans took it over from them.

Wrong: This was an ancient custom among the Greeks and the Romans took it over from them.

Exception

In short sentences made up of clauses closely connected in thought, the comma may be omitted even though the subject of the second clause is different from the first.

Right: He arrived at noon and I took him directly to the hotel.

c) The comma should be omitted between two grammatical elements that are not independent clauses when they are linked by "and," "or," "nor," "but":

Right: This was accomplished by assisting the pupil to clarify her thought and to relate clearly one part of it to another.

Wrong: This was accomplished by assisting the pupil to clarify her thought, and to relate clearly one part of it to another.

Right: The most telling criticism is not of their aims but of their methods.

d) A comma should be used to set off a non-restrictive clause or phrase; no comma should be used to set off a restrictive clause or phrase. An element is non-restrictive if its omission does not alter the meaning of the main part of the sentence.

Right: These books, which are placed on reserve in the Library, are required reading for the course. [The clause is non-restrictive, for the meaning of the main clause is unchanged: "These books are required reading for the course."]

Right: The books which are required reading for this course are placed on reserve in the Library. [The clause is restrictive. The meaning to be conveyed is that the *books which are required reading* are placed on reserve; the others for the course are not on reserve.]

Right: The deserted mill, standing with idle wheel beside the rushing stream, marked the spot where the road turned sharply toward the mountains. [The phrase "standing with idle wheel beside the rushing stream" is merely incidental—that is, non-restrictive.]

Right: The building standing on the site of the old courthouse is the newest in the business section. [Here the phrase "standing on the site of the old courthouse" identifies the building and is therefore restrictive.]

e) Commas should be used to separate the several elements in a simple series (one in which none of the elements contains punctuation within itself) of three or more. It should be noted that a comma should precede the "and" connecting the last two elements but that no comma should follow the final element:

Right: Boston, New York, Chicago, and San Francisco were the cities chosen.

Wrong: Boston, New York, Chicago and San Francisco were the cities chosen.

f) When any of the elements in a series contains within itself commas or other forms of punctuation, the main elements should be separated from one another by semicolons:

Right: The percentages of failures were as follows: Class A, 7 per cent; Class B, 13 per cent; and Class C, 30 per cent.

Right: There are studies of objectives; studies of magazines and newspapers, which are supposed to appeal to young people of this age; studies of the writings of frontier thinkers, some of whom are already familiar figures to the students of American history; and studies of pupil and teacher choices.

g) Commas should be used to set off words or phrases whose function may be described as parenthetical (but see *h* below).

Right: This, however, was not to be borne.
Wrong: This however, was not to be borne.
Wrong: This, however was not to be borne.

h) When a parenthetical expression contains within itself a comma or other form of punctuation, or when it consists of a complete sentence, the preferred style is to use dashes rather than parentheses.

It should be observed that, in typing, a dash consists of two hyphens placed without space between them or at either side.

Right: In the case of Ohio cities of the largest size--that is, Cleveland, Toledo, and Cincinnati--the table shows a definite relation . . .

Right: His record makes it likely--of course it is too early to be certain --that he will receive a scholarship.

i) A dash, not a comma, should precede an appositive coming at the end of a clause and separated from the word or expression it explains:

Right: The state of culture in that institution can be described by only one word—chaos.

Right: Each student kept a record of everything he read—good, bad, and indifferent.

j) A dash should precede a final—summarizing—clause when the subject of the main clause is made up of several elements:

Right: A thousand tragedies and comedies; a score of experiments here and another score there; breathtaking happenings in city, county, state, and nation—all these need the skill of the good student and the good writer.

k) One use of brackets has already been discussed (see sec. 12, *d*, p. 10). A second use is to enclose parenthetical matter within parentheses:

Right: Loammi Baldwin drew attention to the possible deleterious effect of overimmigration . . . (see *Thoughts on Political Economy* [Cambridge, 1809]).

If further parenthesis within the bracket is necessary, parentheses are used again:

Right: The various arguments . . . advanced by Malthus' early American critics (these include certain anonymous writers . . . and Calvin Colton [*Public Economy* (New York, 1848)]) may be formulated as follows.

l) Double quotation marks should be used for a primary quotation whether it contains several words or only one word:

Right: The fact that some things have been called "good" and "bad," "right" and "wrong," sometimes for precisely the same reasons, cannot fail to force itself upon the mind.

Wrong: The fact that some things have been called 'good' and 'bad,' 'right' and 'wrong,' sometimes for precisely the same reasons . . .

Single quotation marks should be used for a quotation within a quotation. Double marks should be used for a third quotation, single again for a fourth, and so on:

Right: Her statement follows: "The man answered: 'Do you think me a fool? The Good Book says, "The fool hath said in his heart, There is no God." I do not acknowledge the existence of a Supreme Being; yet I do not believe I am a fool.' "

When more than one paragraph is quoted, the quotation marks should be placed at the beginning of each paragraph, but at the end of the last paragraph only. In quoting a letter, outline, or similar matter, each item appearing alone on a line should be considered a paragraph and should, therefore, be preceded by quotation marks.[1]

---

[1] This is a general rule for the use of quotation marks. It does not supersede the rule given in section 12, which calls for the indention and single-spacing of long quotations and the omission of quotation marks at beginning and end. In footnotes, however (see sec. 49, p. 49), quoted matter should be enclosed in quotation marks. In text, too, there are times when for the sake of clarity quotation marks should be used to indicate the exact quotation of such matter as outlines, enumerations, etc., which normally would be indented and single-spaced if they were original with the writer of the paper.

Right: "Baltimore, Maryland
                                           "June 1, 1936

    "The University of Chicago
    "Chicago, Illinois
    "Gentlemen:
        "Will you kindly let me have the following information
    concerning . . .
                                           "Very truly yours,
                                           "Clyde L. Brown"

Right: Their outline for the third-year course is as follows:
    "III. Predicate-element concept
    "A. Verb
        "1. Forms and uses of verb 'to be'
        "2. Tense
            "a) Present perfect
            "b) Past perfect"

m) When other marks of punctuation occur in conjunction
with quotation marks, they should be placed according to
the rules set forth in section 12, *e*), (4), page 12.

n) A sentence or a footnote containing either parentheses or
brackets should be punctuated exactly as it would be if the
parentheses or brackets were not there, except that, when
the sentence calls for a mark of punctuation before the
first parenthesis or bracket, it should be omitted at this
point and placed after the second parenthesis or bracket.

Right: The "Diana" might sail for Gibraltar or Tunis (but not
           Malta), where it could pick up a regular Egyptian crew.
Wrong: The "Diana" might sail for Gibraltar or Tunis, (but not Malta),
           where it could pick up a regular Egyptian crew.

Right: Hence springs the whole mass of guardian-spirit myths (with
           some aid from ancestor-worship).
Wrong: Hence springs the whole mass of guardian-spirit myths. (with
           some aid from ancestor-worship)

Right: *Journal of Geology*, XXI (1921), 12.
Wrong: *Journal of Geology*, XXI, (1921) 12.

Interrogation points and exclamation points should be placed inside the parentheses or brackets when they belong to the material so enclosed and not to the whole sentence.

Right: Schleiermacher called it "a feeling of dependence" (a statement which led Hegel to remark that in that case Schleiermacher's dog was more pious than his master!).

When a parenthetical element stands alone (i.e., forms no part of the sentence preceding it), it should begin with a capital and the period should come inside the parenthesis:

Right: All of these ways of validating the claims of religious experience test it by the sources of its authority. (One of the older books introduces a significant distinction between the *organs* of authority and the *source* of authority.)

Appendix III

Sample Pages of a Paper

[Sample Table of Contents of a paper divided into parts as well as into chapters. Division into parts is not necessary (see sec. 9, p. 6). If the chapters are not formally so designated, the word "Chapter" above the column of Roman numerals should be omitted.]

[Sample]

TABLE OF CONTENTS

Page

PART I.   MAN BEFORE CIVILIZATION

Chapter

PART II.   THE ORIGINS AND EARLY HISTORY OF
CIVILIZATION IN THE ANCIENT NEAR EAST

[Sample]

LIST OF TABLES

LIST OF ILLUSTRATIONS[1]

[1] The list of illustrations should be placed on a separate page from the list of tables.

[Sample: First page of a chapter, showing chapter number dropped two inches from upper edge of paper. Double-spaced text and single-spaced footnote.]

CHAPTER II

THE LAND BOOM OF THE RAILROAD ERA, 1843-62

The Period from 1843 to 1848

A new start on the canal.--When the prospect of completing the Illinois and Michigan Canal, apparently involved in the wreck of the state's grandiose scheme of banking and internal improvements, had been abandoned, the death knell of the plans of Chicago to become a great metropolis seemed to have been sounded. The value of its real estate sank to its lowest depths. Of all the projects contemplated by the state, however, the canal, upon which over $7,000,000 had already been spent, was the only one that had been pushed far toward completion. Moreover, it alone possessed in its own right any assets, it still having 230,476 acres of land and 3,491 town lots which had not been sold or mortgaged during the depression.[1] Fortunately for the canal and for Chicago, three different groups found it to their interest to unite to complete the waterway. These were, first, the citizens of Chicago, who fondly expected that the canal would make the city a great emporium; second, the bondholders, who had already sunk their money into the enterprise and who by putting in a little more might recover their entire investment; and, third,

---

[1] James William Putnam, The Illinois and Michigan Canal (Chicago: University of Chicago Press, 1918), p. 58. This is the most authoritative work on the subject of the Illinois and Michigan Canal.

[Sample: One-and-one-half-spaced text, single-spaced footnotes and long quotations, with one-and-one-half spacing between text and quotations and between footnotes.]

Growth of wagon and lake traffic.--While thus being encouraged by the prospects of better transportation facilities in the future, Chicago was forging slowly ahead as a meeting-place of wagon-hauled and lake-borne commerce. Prior to 1837 the territory in the vicinity of Chicago did not raise enough food for its support. That was the first era. Charles Cleaver said:

> From that time to 1842 or 1843 farmers began to raise enough produce for themselves and their neighbors' consumption as well as supplying the citizens of Chicago with all that was necessary, but these years began to show the necessity of having some foreign market to take off the surplus produce, for in the winter of 1842 to 1843 farmers' produce of all kinds was so low it was hardly worth raising. . . . Gradually all classes of produce were held till spring for shipment round the lakes by vessel to New York; this would end the second era.[2]

Notwithstanding the difficulties involved in this long movement by wagons, the volume of wheat thus brought to Chicago rapidly increased. The export of 78 bushels in 1838 had mounted to 40,000 bushels by 1841 and to 587,000 bushels in 1842. Over 1,000,000 bushels were shipped East in 1845 and over 2,000,000 bushels in 1847.[3]

William Bross painted the following picture of Chicago in 1846:

> The residence portion of it [Chicago in 1846] was mainly between Randolph and Madison Streets, and there were some scattered houses as far south as Van Buren Street on the South Side, four or five blocks north of the river on the North Side, with scattering residences about as far on the West Side. There were, perhaps, half a dozen wooden warehouses along the river on Water Street.[4]

---

[2] Charles Cleaver, Reminiscences of Chicago in the Forties and Fifties (Chicago: Fergus Printing Co., 1913), p. 74.

[3] Hunt's Merchants' Magazine, 1858, p. 422.

[4] Chicago Tribune, June 24, 1876.

In 1846, according to Norris, three-fourths of the ground within the city limits was more or less built upon, and there were twenty blocks that were compactly occupied with buildings. There were thirty-two large brick buildings three or four stories in height, and numerous blocks of wooden buildings.[5]

---

[5]Norris, op. cit., p. 5.

Index

Publishing agency, name of, 24

Punctuation, 91–97; of bibliographical entries, 76; of classical references, 41; of footnotes, 20–21; after paragraph headings, 7; with quotation marks, 12; terminal, after headings, omitted, 86

Question marks; *see* Interrogation marks

Quotation marks: double and single, 95; with other punctuation marks, 12; titles of works enclosed in, 29; *see also* Quotations

Quotations: ellipsis in, 9; in footnotes, 49; interpolations in, 10; permissible changes in, 10–12; of poetry, 8; of prose, 8

Radio programs, 75

References in scientific papers, 69–73

Report titles, 28

"Rev.," 16

Review of a book, 35

Roman numerals; *see* Numerals, Roman

Rubber cement, 66

Ruling: of tables, 40; between text and footnotes, 88

Sacred scriptures, 41

Sample pages of a paper, 98–103

Scale of miles, for a map, 65

Scene, of a play, 12, 27

Scientific papers, 52–57; abbreviations in, 73; content footnotes, 73; numerals in, 73–74; organization of, 68; references in, 69–73; symbols in, 73–74

Scriptures, sacred, 29, 41

"Sec." and "secs.," 31

Second or later (footnote) references, 43–47

Secondary-source citation, 43

Semicolon, 91, 93; with quotation marks, 12

Separations; *see* Division of words

Series title, 20, 24, 29

Sermon titles, 29

"*sic*," 10

Spacing: bibliography, 77; box headings, 53; footnotes, and between text and footnotes, 88; "long" quotations, 8; major headings, and between major headings and text, 86; subheadings, 86;

between subheadings and text, 86; table captions, 52; tables, 56; between tables and text, 56; text, 66; between text and footnotes, 88

Spanish: capitalization of titles of works in, 29; ellipsis, 9; underlining of words in, 16, 17

Spelling, 14

Stub column; *see* Tables, stub of

Subheadings, 6, 86–87

"*supra*" 31, 49

Syllabication; *see* Division of words

Symbols, 54, 73–74, 84

Symphony titles, 28

Table of contents, 1, 4, 69

Tables, 50–56, abbreviations in, 54; aligning in columns of, 54; captions for, 52; continuation of, 51; footnotes to, 55; headings of, 53–54; numbering of, 52; oversize, how treated, 51, 52; period leaders in, 54; placement of, 50; ruling, 55–56; spacing, 56; stub of, 54, 55; symbols in, 54

Text, 6–17; abbreviations in, 55–56; chapters or their equivalents in, 6; division of words and other separations in, 15–16; enumerations in, 13–14; foreign words in, 16; introduction a part of, 6; numbers, how expressed in, 12–13; quotations in, 7; sections and subsections in, 6–7; spelling in, 14; titles of works, how treated in, 16

Theses (and dissertations): colored illustrations in, 63; examples of footnote references to, 42; paper for, 84; photographic reproduction of, 63; title pages of, 3; type required for, 83

Time of day, 13, 16

Title page, 1, 3

Titles: abbreviations of, permissible in citing works previously mentioned, 30, 31; capitalization of, 7, 29; in footnotes, when omitted, 30–31; with personal names, 16; of published works, 20, 21, 28, 29; punctuation added to, 22: "quoting" of, 7, 28, 29; in scientific papers, 70; second or later references to, 43–48; underlining of, 7, 28, 29; of unpublished works, 28–29; *see also* Headings

"Total," indented in stub, 54

"Trans.," 31

NOTES

NOTES

NOTES

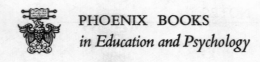

PHOENIX BOOKS
in Education and Psychology

PHOENIX BOOKS
Reference

PHOENIX BOOKS
Literature and Language

PHOENIX BOOKS

in History